All-Color Guide

Rocks and Minerals

Joel Arem

Photographs by Lee Boltin and Joel Arem

G P Geoscience Press, Inc.
Phoenix, Arizona

CO   AUG   '92

Photo Credits
All by Lee Boltin and Joel Arem except p. 122 by Robert Citron,
U.S. National Museum.
Cover: mimetite, South Africa
Title page: calcite

First published as A Bantam Book in 1974
Sixth printing, October 1991   09876

Manufactured in Hong Kong by Hindy's Enterprise
through Jinno International
Cover design by Joanna Hill, Boulder, Colorado

Published by
Geoscience Press, Inc.
12629 N. Tatum Boulevard
Phoenix, Arizona 85032
(602) 953-2330

Contents

1

The Study of Minerals and Rocks

Few subjects are more relevant to our society today than earth science and, specifically, mineralogy. Minerals are among the most precious of our resources. Without knowledge of their use civilization would never have advanced beyond the technology of stone tools. In addition to their economic importance, minerals are endowed with inherent beauty. The study of minerals is therefore both worthwhile and enjoyable.

Rocks are the building blocks of planets and moons. In a strict sense, the study of rocks and minerals is not geology because "ge" is a Latin word meaning "earth." Rocks have been found on the moon and will undoubtedly be collected on the planets as well. Studies of rocks provide information about the origin of the earth and moon, and rock formations are responsible for the scenic beauty of many landscapes.

This book presents the basic information needed to understand what rocks and minerals are, how they form, how they can be identified, and how they are classified. Identification is an acquired skill that improves with practice and experience. After a while you learn to recognize common minerals and rocks at sight, just as you recognize the familiar face of a friend. The many color photographs in this guide are typical of the mineral species they represent, though most of the specimens shown are of higher quality than the average collector is likely to find himself. The localities given for each mineral species are only a few of many worldwide occurrences. Those chosen have produced specimens most familiar to collectors. The color photographs are supplemented by a section on properties useful in identifying minerals. Various tests can be performed with limited equipment, but many give results that are ambiguous and lead to confusion. The tests described are only those which are likely to provide the collector with reliable information.

The section on definitions provides the reader with the necessary background for an understanding of what minerals are and how they form. The same definitions also explain the basic properties of rocks and minerals and lead to a true understanding of crystals and crystal

Rocks are among man's most useful natural resources. Quarries like this produce building stone for a variety of construction projects.

forms. A large table in the back of the book summarizes the mineral properties that can be determined by the amateur and are most useful in identification.

There are between 2,000 and 2,500 mineral species, but only about 150 of them are considered common. Few collectors are able to acquire specimens of even 500 different species, though museums and universities attain such representation. The order in which the minerals are described in this book follows a chemical classification used frequently in large collections. The reader can thus use this book as a guide to mineral exhibits throughout the world.

Minerals are among the most beautiful of nature's creations. They have fascinated man ever since he first began to use stone tools thousands of years ago. They can be collected, displayed, mined, cut into gems, and even eaten (as in the case of salt). Despite their practical uses, minerals reveal their secrets and become truly fascinating only if they are studied. The mineral collector is lucky in that he can learn about minerals in places where they actually form—in road-

cuts, quarries, or any excavation where rocks are exposed. He can then take his specimens home and study them in greater detail. A complete collecting outfit consists merely of a hammer, chisels, knapsack, magnifying glass, heavy gloves, and a notebook for recording observations. Information on where to collect minerals is available in numerous field guides. Maps can be obtained from national, state, and provincial geologic surveys.

Some collectors may wish to cut and polish specimens for display or jewelry, or even make their own mountings. Others like to show their finds at meetings of the numerous mineral and gem clubs that exist throughout the United States and Canada. These clubs sponsor classes, trips, shows, awards, and many other activities. The mineral and gem hobbies rank prominently among popular collecting and craft pastimes. All aspects of these hobbies are enhanced by a deeper understanding of minerals and rocks, their properties and origin.

The first mineralogists were natural historians; minerals, ores, gems, and fossils were all considered in the same category as insects, plants,

Arizona's Grand Canyon, one of the natural **7**
wonders of the world. Chasm dramatizes power of erosional
processes acting through millions of years.

and animals. Today mineralogy is an exact laboratory and field science. The mineralogist shares tools and techniques with ceramists, metallurgists, and chemists. He differs from these other scientists primarily in that he works with naturally occurring materials. The amateur mineralogist plays a vital role in mineralogical research. Although most mineral specimens are recognized through painstaking laboratory investigations, many of these are first brought to the attention of the professional by keen-eyed amateur observers. Many of the best specimens in museums were once owned by nonprofessional mineral enthusiasts. They are beautiful to look at and valuable for research as well.

The geologic concept called *uniformitarianism* states that processes we see at work today, such as the wearing away of rocks at the seashore, have occurred in much the same way throughout geologic time. Thus we can interpret the results of events that took place millions of years ago in terms of observations made today. We can also duplicate geologic processes in the laboratory; by synthesizing minerals a scientist can reveal the conditions of temperature and pressure in which they might have formed in nature. The time factor is very important in geology. Civilizations have grown and vanished in less time than it took to form a tiny quartz crystal.

The science of rocks and minerals is constantly changing. It incorporates bits of chemistry, some physics, some astronomy and mathematics, and a great deal of intuition. Yet in spite of changes in tools, techniques, and sophistication, the basic principles of the science remain the same. At a time when we are realizing that everything in nature is somehow related to everything else, the mineralogist thus finds himself in an excellent position to learn much about the world—and the universe—in which we live.

8   *Niagara Falls (above) and Chiricahua National Monument in Arizona (r.) are continually sculptured by eroding action of water and wind.*

BASIC DEFINITIONS

A **mineral** is a chemical, little different from those you can buy in a jar from a pharmacy, except that bottled chemicals are usually much purer. Part of the definition of a mineral is that it is inorganic (not typical of the chemical matter of living things), and that it occurs naturally. Despite the apparent simplicity of this definition, scientists still disagree on what should or should not be called a mineral. The issue of natural occurrence is one point of contention. For example, at Laurium, Greece, minerals have formed by the reaction of sea water with slags of lead ores. The slags were produced during lead refining more than 2,000 years ago and were dumped into the sea: are the Laurium minerals man-made, or are they natural? A consensus on this problem has not yet been reached.

A **rock** is a solid material that is made up of minerals. This definition allows for rocks that consist of a single mineral (such as limestone, which is composed entirely of the mineral calcite), or of several minerals (such as granite, which typically contains quartz, feldspar, and mica).

Salt (top) is refined from mineral halite. Ores such as chalcopyrite and galena (above) are basic to modern life. Calcite precipitate (r.) at Yellowstone Park.

Rocks make up large structures called *formations*. Many formations are composed of several different types of rocks. The word "formation" also sometimes refers to a particular or characteristic shape taken by a rock mass. The shape reflects the structural properties of the rock, or is the result of *erosional* (wearing away) action of wind and water.

The word *stone*, by itself, has little or no technical meaning. The dictionary definition is "a rock having a specified function" (such as a building stone or gemstone), but otherwise the term should be abandoned in favor of a rock or mineral name.

Ores are minerals from which one or more metals may be extracted at a profit. The idea of monetary gain is essential to the definition of ore. A large deposit of a mineral may be worthless today, but suddenly become ore if the metals it contains increase in value. This has happened many times in the past, especially in the case of metals that had no usefulness until technology found applications for them—such as uranium.

Gems are minerals that have ornamental value. The criteria for deciding if a mineral is a potential gem material are arbitrary, but reasonable, and include such factors as hardness, color, durability, and rarity. Demand for some gems can be created by clever marketing and advertising. Thus, a relatively unknown material can be given popular "gem" stature. "Precious" and "semiprecious" are not scientific or useful terms; at best they can be taken as vague indications of market value.

THE COMPOSITION OF MINERALS

To the uninformed person nature can seem to be a chaotic mass of activity with little apparent organization. But a closer look reveals a profound and elaborate scheme that is organized, structured, and predictable. From the macrocosmic scale (enormous galaxies, solar systems, planets, and moons) to the microcosmic (smaller than the best microscopes can reveal), we find order in nature. At the heart of everything are particles whose existence was imagined by the Greeks more than 2,000 years ago. These early scholars presumed that if one could divide matter fine enough, one would eventually find particles too small to be further split apart. The Greeks called such particles **atoms,** meaning "uncuttable." Today we know that atoms do exist. They are the basic units that make up all matter in the universe.

But atoms are not uncuttable. In fact, they are made up of even smaller particles called **protons, neutrons,** and **electrons.** Scientists

Gems are best-known members of mineral kingdom. Largest one in this array from Smithsonian collection is 287-carat deep-green peridot from Burma.

STRUCTURE OF ATOMS

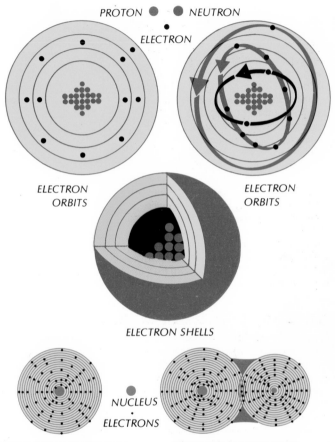

PROTON ● ● NEUTRON

● ELECTRON

ELECTRON ORBITS

ELECTRON ORBITS

ELECTRON SHELLS

● NUCLEUS
· ELECTRONS

ELECTRON DISTRIBUTION IN ATOM

ELECTRON DISTRIBUTION IN MOLECULE

Atoms are made of 3 primary particles: protons, neutrons, electrons. Protons and neutrons inhabit the nucleus, a particle aggregate at center of atom. Electrons are distributed at fixed distances about the nucleus, in "shells," and can be thought of as spinning rapidly about the nucleus.

have found that even these infinitesimal bodies are made of still tinier particles. The smallest of these has yet to be found.

Protons and electrons are charged bodies. An *electric charge* acts in much the same way as the pole of a magnet. It has long been known that "like poles" (such as two north or two south poles) of magnets repel each other, while unlike poles attract. Similarly, like charges (negative-negative or positive-positive) repel and unlike charges attract each other. Electrons have a negative charge and protons have a positive charge. Neutrons are "neutral" and have no charge at all.

Different types of atoms (that is, different **chemical elements**) have different numbers of protons, neutrons, and electrons, but the proton count is the distinguishing factor. In a neutral atom the number of protons is exactly balanced by an equal number of electrons. The positive and negative charges thus cancel exactly, leaving a net charge of zero. Obviously, since neutrons have no charge, their presence does not affect this balance. But neutrons have mass and weigh about as much as protons. Atoms of the same type (having the same number of protons) may have different weights, depending on the number of neutrons present. Such atoms are called **isotopes** of an element. (A list of the chemical elements and their scientific symbols is found on page 144.)

The protons, neutrons, and electrons in atoms (called *subatomic particles* because they are smaller than an atom) are not all lumped together. The protons and neutrons form a central mass, called the **nucleus** of an atom, and the electrons spin about the nucleus. The nucleus has a positive charge (because it contains all the protons) and exerts a very strong attraction on the electrons. To prevent being drawn into the nucleus the electrons spin about it at a very high rate. In fact, they spin so quickly that any given electron seems to be everywhere at once. Atoms are therefore sometimes depicted as a nucleus surrounded by a "cloud" of electrons. The electrons tend to spin about the nucleus at specific distances, but there is a varying degree of probability of finding electrons at various distances from the nucleus. Nonetheless, every electron in an atom contains a specific amount of energy. Because of this fact, electrons can be assigned levels, or *shells,* to which they are restricted. Each shell represents a certain level of energy, which varies with distance from the nucleus.

If you have ever held two powerful magnets close together you know that nothing much happens until the distance between them is very small. Then the attraction becomes so strong it is almost impossible to keep the magnets apart. In atoms, electrons close to the nucleus are attracted very much more intensely than electrons in shells farther away. Outer electrons can be pulled away much more easily than inner electrons. This variation in electron energy accounts for many of the interesting properties of minerals.

The behavior of atoms becomes more readily understandable when they are arranged as Mendeleyev proposed in 1869. Mendeleyev noted that if all the elements were tabulated according to increasing atomic weight (the significance of **atomic number**—that is, the number of protons in an atom—was not yet understood, but weights—that is, protons plus neutrons—could be measured), groups of atoms with similar properties could be distinguished. In fact, such similarities occur with remarkable periodicity or regularity, and a refined version of Mendeleyev's Table is known as the Periodic Table. Atoms on the left side of the table are **metals,** those on the right side are **nonmetals,** and elements exhibiting more variable characteristics are in the middle. But the reasons for the specific behavior of atoms were not clear from considerations only of atomic number; these ultimately were found in studies of the arrangement and behavior of electrons.

IONS AND BONDS

A neutral atom has equal numbers of protons and electrons. Some types of atoms, though, are more stable if they can lose one or more electrons, thereby becoming positively charged. Similarly, other types of atoms tend to gain electrons and become negatively charged. Charged atoms are called **ions** (pronounced eye'-onz); positive ions are *cations* (cat'-eye-onz) and negative ones are called *anions* (an'-eye-onz). In general, metals form cations and nonmetals form anions.

Gain and loss of electrons by atoms is the key to understanding chemical reactions and the properties of all solids, including minerals. Atoms that tend to gain electrons react with atoms that tend to lose electrons. Many chemical processes amount to little more than a transfer of electrons and consequent production of ions. These charged ions attract each other (since opposite electric charges attract) and tend to stick together. The resulting chemical unit is called a **molecule.** Combinations of unlike atoms are called *chemical compounds* and the forces of attraction holding atoms together in compounds are called **bonds.**

The bond between charged atoms is called an *ionic bond* because charged atoms are ions. In an ionic bond electrons have actually left one atom and transferred to another. Sometimes, though, electrons are not completely lost by an atom but are shared with one or more

15

IONS AND BONDS

+ ←————→ +
Like Charges Repel

+ ——✕—— −
Unlike Charges Attract

Ionic Bond

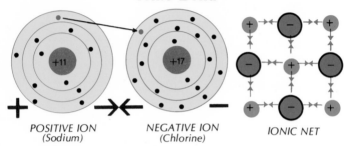

+ ——✕—— **−**

POSITIVE ION
(Sodium)

NEGATIVE ION
(Chlorine)

IONIC NET

Metallic Bond

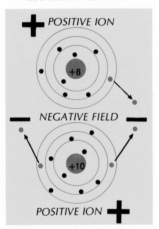

+ POSITIVE ION

+8

— NEGATIVE FIELD **—**

+10

POSITIVE ION **+**

Covalent Bond

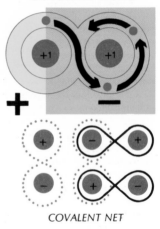

+1   +1

+   **−**

COVALENT NET

*Types of bonds differ in the way electrons
are distributed about atoms. In ionic bonds electrons are transferred
from one atom to another, producing a charge on
both atoms (then termed ions). In metals, atoms are positive ions
in a "sea" of loosely held electrons. In
covalent bonding, electrons are shared by 2 or more atoms.*

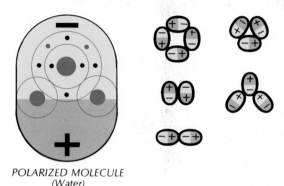

VAN DER WAALS BOND

POLARIZED MOLECULE
(Water)

Van der Waals bonds are weak forces caused by irregularities
in electron distribution within atoms and molecules.
The result is a separation of positive and negative charges,
allowing such molecules to bond to other molecules or atoms.

other atoms. The atoms then engage in a kind of "tug-of-war" with the electrons, no atom winning or losing them entirely. The result is a very strong link between the atoms, called a *covalent bond* (cohvay'-lent). The very term "covalent" implies electron sharing.

Other types of bonds also exist. In metals, for instance, the atoms are packed tightly together and electrons are more or less free to wander among them. The forces holding the metal atoms together are called *metallic bonds*. The loose attachment of the individual metals to their electrons accounts for the good electrical conductivity and heat conductivity of these substances.

Another type of bond, called the *Van der Waals bond* (after a Dutch chemist) is an extremely weak force of attraction between essentially neutral atoms. Van der Waals bonds result in distinct planes of weakness along which materials break very easily, as for example in the mica minerals.

Bonding is important in determining mineral properties. It also affects the way in which atoms and molecules join together. In special cases, namely in solids, bond forces result in a geometrically arranged aggregate of atoms. These aggregates are called crystals.

2
Crystals and Their Structures

All minerals are either elements or chemical compounds. Their properties depend largely on the types of bonds holding their atoms together. Most minerals are solids (as opposed to liquids and gases) with a distinguishing feature—*long-range order*—that accounts for many of their characteristics.

Long-range order simply means that the atoms and molecules of a solid are not jumbled together randomly, but are arranged in a pattern. In gases and liquids the atoms are moving about so rapidly that they never stay in one place long enough to establish patterns. But in solids the atoms and molecules are locked by strong chemical bonds into rigid arrays. Every atom in a solid has definite neighbors at specific distances. In addition, every similar atom in the solid has the same types of neighbors and in the same relative positions. A material organized in this way is said to be *crystalline*. All solids are, by definition, crystalline. A **crystal** is merely a mass of crystalline material that is bounded by natural growth surfaces. The external shape of a crystal is called its *habit*. The general study of crystal forms is called *morphology*.

The surfaces of a crystal do not have to be plane, shiny, and smooth. One may speak of **anhedral** crystals (having no plane faces at all), **subhedral** crystals (having crude geometric shape or form), and **euhedral** crystals (bounded by plane faces). A crystal is a crystal because of the way its atoms are arranged. In a sense, the flat, smooth external faces of euhedral crystals are an "accident" of crystal growth.

Twin crystals are crystals that are intergrown in a characteristic way. Many minerals form essentially random clusters, where crystals have interfered with each other during growth. A twin, however, consists of two or more crystals of the same mineral intersecting on planes or lines that are significant with respect to the structure of the mineral. *Twin laws* refer to characteristic twin relationships that are frequently observed. Descriptive terms for twins generally refer to twin laws or to the external shape of twin crystals.

The term *crystal structure* implies the presence of atoms of specific types, arranged in an orderly way. Structural patterns are geometrical.

Calcite from Cumberland, England, is among the most beautiful of all minerals. Its crystals are highly prized by discerning collectors.

The simplest example familiar to most people is probably wallpaper, in which a design is repeated at intervals in two dimensions (the plane of the paper). In solids the patterns are three-dimensional, but the principle of design repetition is the same as in wallpaper. In crystals the repeated design is called a *motif*.

Motifs in crystals are groups of atoms. An atomic motif can be very complex and irregular, or as regular and geometrical as a square wallpaper design. The importance of motifs in crystals is that they are repeated regularly in three dimensions. If you imagine every motif replaced by a single dot, and then connect all the dots in straight rows, you create a network of lines with regular spacings between them. This is a kind of scaffolding or framework that indicates the arrangement of the motifs; it is called a *lattice*.

A crystal structure consists of the lattice arrangement combined with the shape of the atomic motifs. Every structure thus has two independent types of patterns in it: that of the lattice and that of the motif. Because of the special geometrical nature of lattices and their properties, only 14 different types of lattices are possible. Among these, only seven basic shapes can be distinguished because several types have the same shape as others. In addition, two of the seven "unique" shapes actually can be considered the same lattice looked at in different ways. So we are left with six different basic lattice types to form the structures of all solids, including minerals. These lattices give us six **crystal systems.**

In each lattice type we can find a closed box whose shape indicates the geometrical characteristics of the lattice itself. Considering one corner of this box as a starting point, we can distinguish three edges whose directions are called the *axes* of the lattice. The lengths of the box edges define the basic dimensions of the lattice.

In the **isometric system** the axes are all the same length and are

*External form of crystals (above, l. to r.): anhedral—
no faces; subhedral—indistinct faces; euhedral—flat, well-formed
faces. Quartz from Japan (r.) illustrates twinning of crystals.*

all at right angles to one another. This results in a "unit box" in the shape of a cube. In the **tetragonal system** the axes are all at right angles, but one axis is a different length from the other two.

The **orthorhombic system** has axes all at right angles, but the dimensions of the unit box are all different; orthorhombic lattices are thus built of brick-shaped units.

In the **monoclinic system** two axes are at right angles to each other and the third makes some angle with the other two; all the axes can be different lengths. In the **triclinic system** there are no restrictions on either the lengths of the axes or the angles between them. In the **hexagonal system** there are two axes that make an angle of 120 degrees and a third axis at right angles to the other two. The axes intersecting at 120 degrees are of equal length, and the third is a different length. People often think of the hexagonal system as having three axes in a plane that meet at 60 degrees, but the third planar axis is not required to describe the lattice. (The so-called *rhombohedral lattice* or rhombohedral system is merely another way of looking at a hexagonal lattice.)

Symmetry can be thought of as a repetition of appearance or properties. Symmetry results in the repetition of *crystal faces*, which are flat surfaces that sometimes form the outer boundaries of well-formed

INTERNAL STRUCTURE OF CRYSTALS

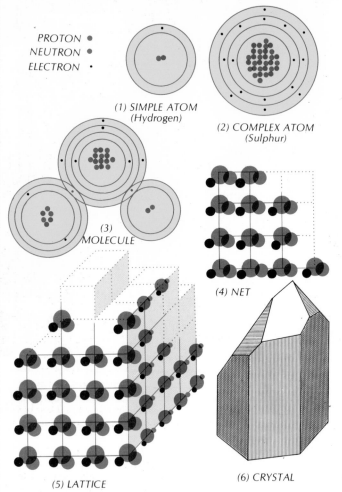

PROTON ●
NEUTRON ●
ELECTRON ·

(1) SIMPLE ATOM
(Hydrogen)

(2) COMPLEX ATOM
(Sulphur)

(3) MOLECULE

(4) NET

(5) LATTICE

(6) CRYSTAL

Crystals are made of atoms that are
arranged in patterns. Simple and complex atoms join to form
molecules. Two-dimensional arrays of
molecules are called "nets." Nets stacked in 3 dimensions
form "lattices." Even the tiniest crystal
contains many thousand lattice units.

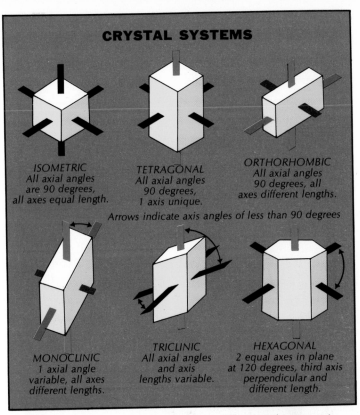

CRYSTAL SYSTEMS

ISOMETRIC
All axial angles
are 90 degrees,
all axes equal length.

TETRAGONAL
All axial angles
90 degrees,
1 axis unique.

ORTHORHOMBIC
All axial angles
90 degrees, all
axes different lengths.

Arrows indicate axis angles of less than 90 degrees

MONOCLINIC
1 axial angle
variable, all axes
different lengths.

TRICLINIC
All axial angles
and axis
lengths variable.

HEXAGONAL
2 equal axes in plane
at 120 degrees, third axis
perpendicular and
different length.

crystals. *Axial symmetry* is the repetition of features about an axis. *Plane symmetry* acts like a mirror and repeats features on opposite sides of a flat plane. A *center of symmetry* repeats points on opposite sides of a crystal, diagonally through the center. Crystals with "high symmetry" contain many such symmetry elements—planes, axes, and centers.

Since lattices can be thought of in terms of unit boxes, their chief characteristics are expressed in lengths (of box edges) and angles (between crystal axes). Unit distances between lattice points are called *translations,* and lattices thus have *translational symmetry* which repeats objects at equal distances through space. Motifs, on the other hand, are clusters of atoms or molecules; these are distributed about a point. This distribution results in *point symmetry,* the repetition of

PLANE SYMMETRY

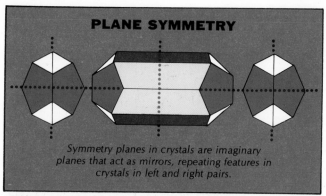

Symmetry planes in crystals are imaginary planes that act as mirrors, repeating features in crystals in left and right pairs.

AXIAL SYMMETRY

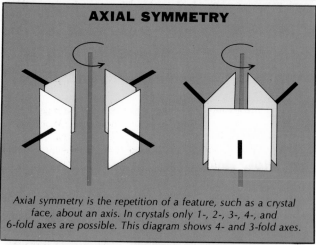

Axial symmetry is the repetition of a feature, such as a crystal face, about an axis. In crystals only 1-, 2-, 3-, 4-, and 6-fold axes are possible. This diagram shows 4- and 3-fold axes.

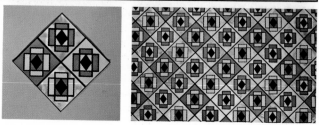

24   Like unit repeated in wallpaper design (bottom), crystal "motifs" are repeated, but in three dimensions. Model (opposite) is typical silicate mineral structure.

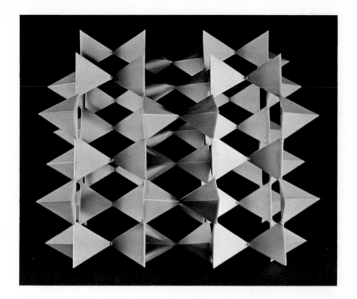

features (or atoms) at various places about a point. This type of symmetry includes axes, planes, and centers, as mentioned above. When symmetry operations—such as reflection across a plane or rotation about an axis—are combined in a single group of atoms, the operations act on each other as well (for example, a fourfold symmetry axis could repeat a symmetry plane four times about itself). There are limitations to the number of possible combinations of point symmetries, resulting in 32 distinct groups. These provide us with 32 *crystal classes*. Crystal systems are thus based on lattice symmetry, while the crystal classes are derived from motif (point) symmetry.

Symmetry is important for several reasons. It enables us to determine the crystal system to which a mineral belongs, because lattices have certain basic symmetries. The physical properties of minerals vary with the types of bonding present. But bonds are repeated through a crystal in a symmetrical way. The physical properties of a mineral are thus every bit as symmetrical as the external form. Some "bulk" properties are primarily chemical rather than physical in nature, in that they depend on the types of atoms present rather than the atomic structure. Bulk properties are thus independent of structure, but most physical properties are structure-dependent.

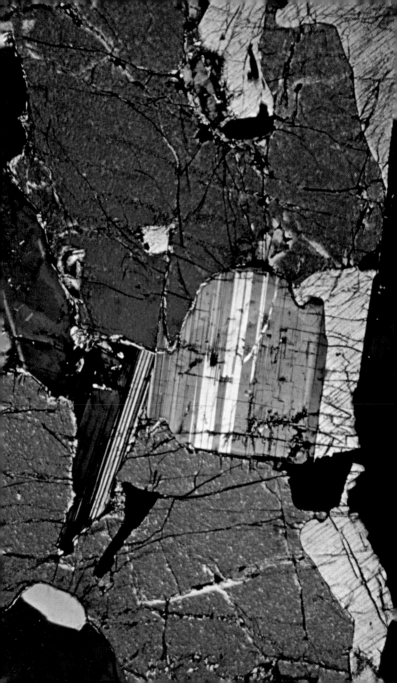

3
The Properties of Minerals

Identification of minerals is based on their physical and chemical properties. Some of these properties are variable even for a single mineral, depending on the location and conditions in which the mineral formed. Thus, a chemical test may not give clear, unambiguous results. Chemical elements with similar atomic size and charge can substitute for each other in a mineral structure, and identification often means determining which element is present in largest amount. This may require precise laboratory analysis. One test alone should never be used to identify a mineral. Sometimes even a combination of tests is not sufficient and sophisticated laboratory equipment must be used, including X-ray, optical, and chemical devices.

X-rays are useful in identifying minerals. A beam of X-rays passed through a mineral fragment or crystal is split up into many smaller beams. These emerge in a pattern that is characteristic of the symmetry of the specimen. A *powder photograph* records the pattern of emerging X-ray beams; it can be measured to give data on the structure of the mineral and the size of its lattice. Very sophisticated X-ray machines are used to determine the actual atomic structures of crystals.

Expensive laboratory equipment is not required to identify most common minerals. Much can be done by the amateur with simple tools, such as a magnet, knife, and magnifying glass. The properties described on the following pages are easy to determine and are usually sufficient to identify any mineral the average collector is likely to find. Chemical tests can sometimes be useful, but they are often misleading or ambiguous and should always be used in combination with other tests. Sight identification is a powerful technique, but only in the hands of an experienced collector; the photographs in this book will provide a guide to the typical appearance of many minerals. The easily determined properties are summarized in a large table at the back of the book which is arranged alphabetically by species. Once an idea as to the identity of a mineral is attained, checking the table will rapidly eliminate incorrect guesses. The collector should always try to identify his own specimens, for constant practice is the only way to become proficient at recognizing minerals.

"Thin section," ultrafine slice of rock, lets light through. Colors are due to polarizing effects. Specimen is olivine diabase from Elfdalen, Sweden.

28   *Electron microprobe X-ray analyzer (top) reveals
chemical composition of minerals; X-ray powder cameras (above)
identify them. Author measures X-ray powder photo (r.).*

BULK PROPERTIES

The relative weight or ''heft'' of a mineral is measured against the weight of water, and the measurement is called its **specific gravity** (S.G.). For example, a mineral weighing 3½ times the weight of an equal volume of water has a specific gravity (or *density*) of 3.5. The measurement of S.G. is arrived at by a simple test. First carefully note the dry weight of a mineral fragment. Then take the weight of the fragment while it is totally immersed in water. While submerged, it will seem to weigh less than it did in air, due to buoyancy. At the same time it will displace a volume of water equal to its own volume. The weight of the displaced water is the same as the difference between the weight of the fragment in air and its weight in water. To obtain the S.G. of the mineral, divide the dry weight of the fragment by the weight of the displaced water. The mineral's specific gravity is thus calculated as follows:

$$S.G. = \frac{Weight\ in\ air}{Weight\ of\ equal\ volume\ of\ water} = \frac{Weight\ in\ air}{Loss\ of\ weight\ in\ water}$$

Luster is the way a mineral surface reflects light. Except in the case of metals, luster does not affect the color of a mineral. Minerals are generally classified according to whether they have a metallic or non-metallic luster. Nonmetallic lusters are subdivided as follows, with examples in parentheses:

Minerals variously reflecting light are displaying degree of luster. This property depends on orientation of specimen, can vary within a single mineral.

Vitreous—the luster of glass (quartz, apatite, tourmaline)

Resinous—the luster of resin, such as amber (sphalerite)

Greasy—as if covered with a layer of grease or oil (nepheline, serpentine, some quartz)

Pearly—the iridescent sheen of mother-of-pearl (talc, mica, apophyllite)

Silky—the lustrous, fibrous sheen of rayon or silk (fibrous gypsum, asbestos)

Adamantine—the hard, brilliant flash of a diamond (diamond, cassiterite, corundum, cerussite)

Dull—a surface showing little reflectivity (leucite)

Earthy—the powdery, crumbly look of compacted soil (kaolin, limonite)

Streak is the color of a powdered mineral. It is seen by rubbing a specimen against a piece of unglazed porcelain (such as a bathroom tile), which is called for this purpose a *streak plate*. Usually the mineral will crumble and leave a trail of powder whose color can easily be noted. Many minerals have a white streak, and other minerals have characteristic streaks whose color differs from that of the mineral itself. Examples are:

Mineral	Mineral Color	Streak color
Bornite	Brassy yellow	Gray-black
Chalcopyrite	Brassy yellow	Greenish-black
Cinnabar	Red	Scarlet
Hematite	Black, brown, red	Red
Limonite	Brownish yellow	Rusty yellow-brown
Pyrite	Brassy yellow	Black
Siderite	Brown, green	White
Zincite	Deep red	Orange

30 *Test for streak—the color of a powdered mineral—is to rub mineral against unglazed porcelain plate (l.). Scratch (r.) is crude measure of mineral hardness.*

SPECIFIC GRAVITY

SPECIMEN IN AIR

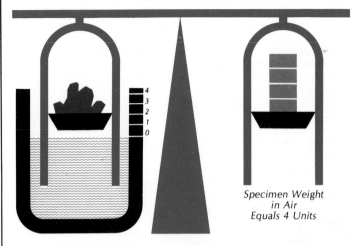

Specimen Weight
in Air
Equals 4 Units

SPECIMEN IN WATER

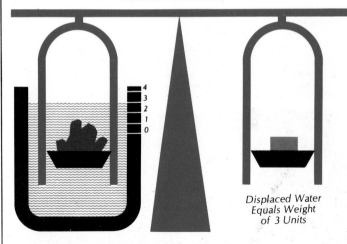

Displaced Water
Equals Weight
of 3 Units

*The specific gravity of an object is its weight
compared to that of an equal volume of water. The ratio is obtained
by measuring the weight of water which the object displaces.*

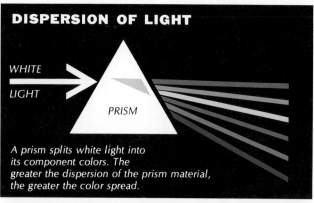

DISPERSION OF LIGHT

WHITE
LIGHT

PRISM

A prism splits white light into
its component colors. The
greater the dispersion of the prism material,
the greater the color spread.

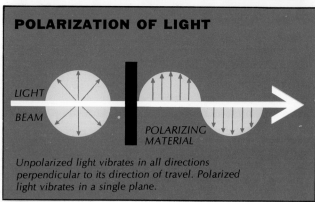

POLARIZATION OF LIGHT

LIGHT
BEAM

POLARIZING
MATERIAL

Unpolarized light vibrates in all directions
perpendicular to its direction of travel. Polarized
light vibrates in a single plane.

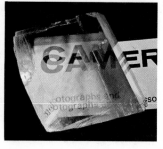

*Film exposed to radioactive mineral (above l.) "takes
its picture." Optical property of double refraction (above r.)
results from splitting light paths within specimen.*

Radioactivity and **magnetism** are easily detected properties of minerals. Some elements (such as uranium and thorium) emit radiations of various kinds. These are known as *alpha particles* (clumps made of two protons and two neutrons), *beta particles* (high-energy electrons), and *gamma rays* (powerful and penetrating radiations). Gamma rays can be stopped only by thick layers of dense materials such as lead.

Uranium and thorium minerals are radioactive because atoms of these elements spontaneously break apart to produce alpha, beta, and gamma radiation. This radiation can be detected by special instruments called Geiger and scintillation counters. A *Geiger counter* contains a gas-filled tube with a wire running down the center. Radiation entering the tube reacts with the gas and sends a pulse of electric current down the wire. The pulses can be counted, giving a measure of the amount of radiation present. A *scintillation counter* contains a special crystal that gives off a flash of light when struck by radiation; the flashes are amplified and counted. A uranium prospector's chief tool is a Geiger counter. Its readings tell him when he is close to ore.

Magnetism is present in only a few minerals, and so the property is a key aid in identification. A strong pocket magnet (such as an Alnico type) will pick up bits of magnetite (iron oxide) and pyrrhotite (iron sulfide), as well as some other iron and nickel minerals. Lodestone is a variety of magnetite that is itself a natural magnet able to pick up bits of iron. Lodestone is undoubtedly the source of magnetism used by the earliest seafaring people to make compasses for navigation.

Specific gravity, streak, radioactivity, and magnetism are all "bulk" properties of minerals, in that they do not vary with orientation of a specimen. Other properties, however, depend on crystal symmetry. The regularity in atomic arrangement in mineral structures is displayed in both the repetition of crystal faces and in the repetition of equivalent chemical bonds in different directions. Since bonds largely determine the properties of minerals, it follows that many properties must also be symmetrical. The next pages describe structure-dependent mineral characteristics.

COLOR AND OPTICAL PROPERTIES

All crystals affect the behavior of light that passes through them. Light is a wave-like form of energy that normally vibrates in all planes perpendicular to its direction of travel. *Polarized light* is light that has been forced to vibrate in a single plane. When polarized light is passed through a transparent fragment of a mineral, it produces characteristic colors that can be used to identify the mineral. This technique requires the use of *thin sections* (slices of rocks and minerals so thin that light can pass through them, about 0.003 inch). The device most commonly used to study such materials is called a *polarizing microscope*.

Light travels through space at a constant rate of 186,000 miles per second and is not much slowed by air. But in passing through liquids and solids, it is both slowed and forced to change its path. This bending is what makes a pencil held in a glass of water appear bent or broken. The degree to which light is slowed down in a material is called the **index of refraction** of the material; it is measured in terms of the angular change in light path associated with the change in speed. Refractive index varies with direction in crystals, and all substances except isometric materials have more than one index of refraction. The change in light path creates brilliance in properly cut gems. Measurement of refractive indices is an exact science and provides a great deal of information about crystals.

Light that appears to be white (such as sunlight) actually is made up of a mixture of light of all colors. Most objects tend to absorb one or more of the color components of white light, and the color we see is actually that of the remaining light that reaches our eyes. A red object appears red because it absorbs all the colors in white light *except* red.

Different colors are absorbed by a crystal when light passes through it in different directions. This effect (called **pleochroism**) explains the color changes often observed when a mineral is viewed in different

34

Mica (top l.) cleaves along specific planes.
Conchoidal fracture (above l.) is typical of quartz and glass.
Ultraviolet light produces glow of fluorescence.

directions (as in tourmaline and spodumene). Since color in most minerals is due to absorption of light, thicker pieces of material absorb more light and give deeper colors. Some minerals are nearly always the same color (azurite—blue; malachite—green; sulfur—yellow; cinnabar—red), but even these colors are slightly variable. For example, the layers in banded malachite are different shades of green. In general, color is not a good property to use in identifying minerals and should never be relied on as a sole test. Color does, of course, provide some clues, but one should always examine a freshly broken surface. The surface color of a mineral may be due to tarnish or weathering and be very different from the true color (good examples are bornite and siderite). Sometimes surface color or tarnish is also an aid in identification, as in the case of bornite ("peacock ore").

Fluorescence and Phosphorescence

In some minerals the electrons surrounding particular atoms can change their orbits around the nucleus, such as by moving farther away from the nucleus and spinning at a greater distance from it. For this to happen, energy must be supplied. Ultraviolet light (the part of the sun's radiation that causes sunburn) is one such energy source. When ultraviolet light strikes a mineral it may cause electrons in the structure to change orbits. Later these electrons return to their original positions and give up the energy they absorbed, releasing it in the form of light and creating an effect called **fluorescence.** If there is some delay (perhaps even hours or days) in the electrons' return to their original orbits, the fluorescent light will be emitted over a similar period of time. This effect is called **phosphorescence.** A mineral that emits fluorescent or phosphorescent light is called a **phosphor.** Phosphors can be manufactured at low cost, and their use makes possible such devices as fluorescent light bulbs and color television sets.

Collecting fluorescent minerals is a very exciting specialty. Portable ultraviolet lamps make it possible to detect fluorescence in the field, usually at night, and displays of fluorescent minerals are particularly attractive.

MECHANICAL PROPERTIES

The way a mineral breaks depends largely on the bonds holding its atoms together. If planes of weakness exist in a mineral structure between layers of atoms joined by weak bonds, the mineral will tend to separate on these planes. This property is called **cleavage.** Where no distinct planes of weakness exist, breakage occurs in a less regular fashion and is termed **fracture.** All minerals display fracture, but not all minerals show good cleavage. When planes of weakness exist in a structure but cleavage is not demonstrated by all specimens of the material, the tendency for splitting to occur along planes is called *parting.* Cleavage is ranked as poor, fair, good, perfect, or eminent. Fracture is described as conchoidal, fibrous, splintery, hackly, even, and uneven. Conchoidal fracture resembles the concentric circular lines on the surfaces of many beach shells. (The name is from Greek words meaning "shell form.") This type of fracture is seen commonly on glass and quartz.

Since structures are symmetrical, planes of weakness are repeated by symmetry. Some minerals break into perfect cubes, indicating that the internal symmetry of these minerals is cubic. Cleavage is thus a good indication of the internal arrangement of the atoms in a mineral.

Hardness varies with the method of measurement used. To the mineralogist, hardness is simply the resistance of a material to being scratched. A scratch is a small furrow plowed into the surface of a solid. In the scratching process, bonds between atoms are broken. Resistance to scratching depends on the strength of the atomic bonds. Hardness is thus related to bonding and structure, and is a symmetrical property of crystals.

The standard test for hardness involves scratching one mineral with another. A material is considered harder than any other mineral it will scratch. A table suggested by Friedrich Mohs (the *Mohs scale*) is in widespread use. It lists some common minerals in order of increas-

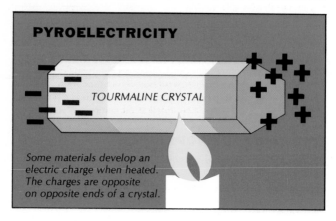

PYROELECTRICITY

TOURMALINE CRYSTAL

Some materials develop an electric charge when heated. The charges are opposite on opposite ends of a crystal.

ing hardness. A mineral with a higher hardness number will scratch any mineral with a lower number. Diamond (10) is the hardest natural substance and will scratch any other mineral.

Mohs' Scale				
1 Talc	**3** Calcite	**5** Apatite	**7** Quartz	**9** Corundum
2 Gypsum	**4** Fluorite	**6** Orthoclase	**8** Topaz	**10** Diamond

Some common materials are useful in testing hardness and have the following Mohs-scale values: Fingernail: 2.5; Copper penny: 3–4; Knife blade: 5.5; Window glass: 5.5; Steel file: 6.5.

ELECTRICAL PROPERTIES

Crystals belonging to certain low-symmetry classes may exhibit completely different forms and properties at opposite ends. A good example of this is found in such minerals of the tourmaline group as elbaite, schorl, and dravite. The tourmalines display both piezoelectricity and pyroelectricity. **Piezoelectricity** is the production of an electric current in crystals subjected to pressure. This principle is the basis of the phonograph, in which a piezoelectric crystal converts vibrations (through the needle in a record groove) to an electric current, which is then converted to sound. Quartz and Rochelle salt (not a mineral) are both widely used piezoelectric materials.

Pyroelectricity is the development of an electric charge in a crystal due to a change in temperature. Tourmaline crystals tend to gather dust due to this effect.

Mineral properties are quite variable. Hardness may depend on the physical perfection of the material and whether it is a single crystal or an aggregate. Luster varies with orientation even in a single specimen. The composition of a mineral can be drastically affected by the presence of impurities. Specific gravity is altered by impurities, microscopic flaws, cracks, and bubbles. Few mineral properties are so constant that simple tests always provide positive identification. The collector must always consider which tests are useful and which ones are likely to be ambiguous, and this often depends on the problem at hand. Looking at many specimens (opportunities exist in most places to visit museums that have mineral displays) and consulting the descriptions in this guide will lead to rapid familiarity with many common mineral species.

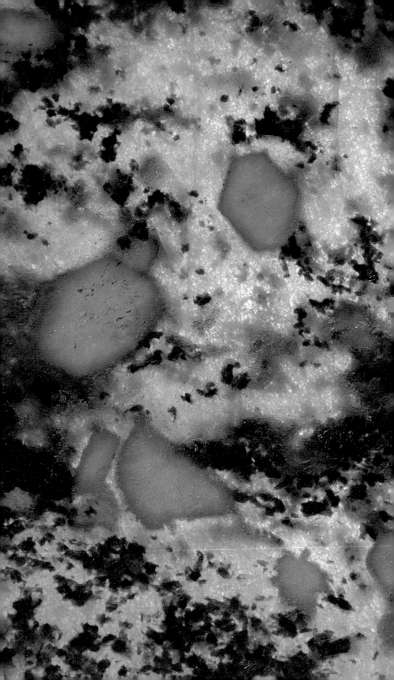

4
Classifying Minerals

There is no single "best" way to arrange minerals for storage or study. The critical requirement is accessibility. You must be able to find specimens when you want them. The collector who arranges his minerals alphabetically is as correct as any advocate of a chemical or structural system.

One finds, however, that most large collections, especially in universities and museums, are arranged according to the **Dana classification.** This is a choice based on historical precedent. In 1850 James D. Dana published his *System of Mineralogy,* a reference work which classified minerals according to their chemical composition. It became widely accepted, and many editions of the *System* have since appeared. Dana's scheme continues in use by weight of tradition, although other methods of classification have been devised.

Any convenient arrangement of minerals is suitable for the beginner. But since advanced texts and collections use the Dana scheme and similar classification systems, it is a great advantage to become familiar with these systems at an early stage. For this reason the minerals discussed on the following pages are presented in a sequence closely matching the Dana order.

Crystal chemistry is a branch of science that relates the chemical composition, physical properties, and internal structure of crystalline materials. In minerals certain types of atomic arrangements occur with great regularity and frequency. These arrangements provide a logical system for describing and classifying minerals.

Atoms of nonmetals are very much larger than those of metals. In crystals the nonmetal atoms are packed together quite tightly, but there is enough space between them for metal atoms to fit in. A specific kind of metal tends always to fit spaces of the same size and shape and thus be surrounded by a fairly consistent arrangement of nonmetals. One can think of such an atomic cluster as a unit, called a **radical** or a **coordination polyhedron** (a polyhedron is a multisided, geometrical shape). The metal is at the center of the polyhedron and the nonmetal atoms form the corners. For example, a silicon atom tends always to surround itself with four atoms of oxygen, forming a tetrahedron

Brilliant red ruby crystals contrast with green chrome zoisite matrix in this specimen from Tanzania.

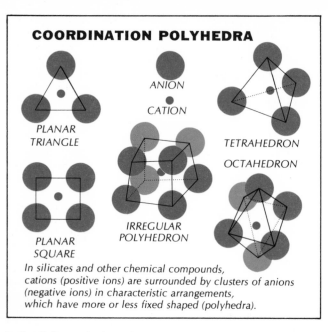

COORDINATION POLYHEDRA

PLANAR TRIANGLE

ANION
CATION

PLANAR SQUARE

IRREGULAR POLYHEDRON

TETRAHEDRON

OCTAHEDRON

In silicates and other chemical compounds,
cations (positive ions) are surrounded by clusters of anions
(negative ions) in characteristic arrangements,
which have more or less fixed shaped (polyhedra).

(a closed shape with four sides). Atoms of magnesium, iron, and many other metals tend to prefer the space inside a cluster of six oxygen atoms in the shape of an octahedron. Such polyhedra are found in many minerals. The consistent appearance of specific polyhedra makes classification according to such atomic groups both logical and practical.

The Dana scheme classifies minerals in the following general order:

1. Native elements	7. Nitrates
2. Sulfides	8. Borates
3. Sulfosalts	9. Sulfates; Chromates
4. Oxides; Hydroxides	10. Phosphates; Vanadates; Arsenates
5. Halides	11. Tungstates; Molybdates
6. Carbonates	12. Silicates

These classes are further subdivided into families, groups, species, and varieties according to similarities in structure and variations in chemistry. The first five groups above vary widely in structural arrangement and chemistry, whereas groups 6 through 12 are characterized by a specific coordination polyhedron. These will be described individually in the following pages. The specific minerals illustrated are among the most common minerals likely to be encountered by the collector. In most cases only a few localities are indicated (the ones best known to collectors), although the mineral may occur in thousands of localities throughout the world. Mineral properties and chemical formulas are given in the table beginning on page 145.

NATIVE ELEMENTS

Native elements are those found uncombined chemically in nature. Included in this group are metals, nonmetals, and semimetals (which exhibit characteristics of both metals and nonmetals). The hardest, softest, and most costly minerals are also native elements.

The gold group is made up of gold, silver, and copper. All three metals were known to early civilizations, and have played a major role in human history. Gold and silver have always been prized for their beauty and scarcity. Copper is an important industrial metal.

Metals can be melted together to form mixtures called **alloys.** Alloys of copper with zinc (brass) and with tin (bronze) were very important materials more than 5,000 years ago, though they are less in use today. Silver frequently occurs naturally alloyed with gold, mercury, and copper. Much of the silver mined today is used in making photographic emulsions, as well as in coinage, jewelry, and industrial processes. Gold is generally hoarded. It forms the basis of most of the world's currencies and is used in jewelry and in technical applications.

The platinum group consists of platinum, iridium, osmium, and palladium. All have high specific gravities (osmium is the heaviest element). Platinum is used in jewelry and is also a chemical *catalyst* (a substance that speeds up chemical reactions without itself participating in the reactions). A few semimetals (arsenic, bismuth, and antimony) occur in the native state, but are rare. Iron is also rare on earth as a native element, but large iron-nickel alloy masses occur in meteorites.

The nonmetals carbon and sulfur are very important. Sulfur is used in fertilizers, explosives, rubber, paper, and insecticides and in manufacturing sulfuric acid, a key industrial chemical. Carbon occurs in two native forms: graphite and diamond. Graphite is one of the softest known substances and is used as a lubricant. Diamond, the hardest known substance, is used as an abrasive and as a gemstone. The vast difference in hardness between diamond and graphite is due to the differing structural arrangement and bonding of carbon atoms.

GOLD occurs in native form in many parts of the world. It is found in veins formed at high temperatures associated with quartz and certain sulfides. Weathering and erosion of gold-bearing rocks frees the gold, which is nearly *inert* (chemically unreactive) and is eventually reduced to fine particles by rolling in streams. It collects in curves in stream beds because of its high specific gravity. Such concentrations form *placer deposits* of gold; some of the largest gold mines in the world are associated with stream sediments. *Nuggets* are large, waterworn fragments of native metal. *Loc:* Alaska; California—mother lode; South Dakota; Siberia—placer; South Africa (Witwatersrand); Australia.

SILVER is more abundant than gold and does form chemical compounds (with oxygen and sulfur) in nature. Native silver often forms spectacular crystals, wires, and sheets. Silver is usually obtained as a by-product of the refining of ores of other metals (in which it occurs in minor amounts). Nuggets of copper-silver alloy are called *half-breeds*. Silver occurs principally in veins with gold, or with ores of lead and zinc, in low-temperature deposits. *Loc:* Canada (Cobalt, Ontario); Colorado; Arizona; Michigan (Keeweenaw Peninsula); Mexico; Norway (Kongsberg); Australia (Broken Hill, NSW).

COPPER in native form is mined extensively in but one place, the Keeweenaw Peninsula, Michigan, where it occurs in volcanic rocks called basalt (see p. 127); Michigan copper was used by American Indians thousands of years ago. Crystals of native copper are sometimes quite large, and masses of several tons are known from the Michigan mines. Some of these were too large to move and still remain in the old mines. Native copper sometimes occurs in the oxidized portions of sulfide ore bodies. *Loc:* Michigan (Keeweenaw Peninsula); Arizona; New Mexico; South-West Africa (Tsumeb); England (Cornwall); Mexico; U.S.S.R.

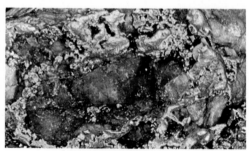

42

Above: Gold and quartz—Va. Opposite: Silver—Kongsberg, Norway (top); Copper—Keeweenaw Peninsula, Mich. (bottom).

DIAMOND typically occurs in crystals, usually deformed octahedra and tetrahedra, and in a wide variety of colors. Industrial-grade diamonds are often discolored, rounded, or black and termed *bort, ballas,* or *carbonado* respectively. Diamonds form in conditions of very high temperature and pressure, deep within the earth, in circular, pipe-like formations of igneous rocks called **kimberlite.** Diamond pipes have been found in several countries. For many years India was the only source of diamonds. The largest diamond ever found weighed over 3,000 carats (about 1⅓ pounds) and gems cut from it are the world's largest. *Loc:* India; Brazil; U.S.S.R.; British Guiana; Venezuela; South Africa; Arkansas (Murfreesboro); Australia.

GRAPHITE is used chiefly as a lubricant, but is also familiar as the "lead" in lead pencils. Graphite is in such great demand that natural sources are insufficient, and the mineral is manufactured in electric furnaces. Graphite "brushes" are found in most electric motors; graphite crucibles are used in very-high-temperature applications; the mineral is also used to absorb neutrons in nuclear reactors. *Loc:* New York (Adirondack region); Alabama; New Mexico; Mexico; Ceylon; Madagascar; Siberia; Bavaria; Canada.

SULFUR occurs in many parts of the world associated with salt in immense, dome-shaped deposits. Fine crystals, however, come from only a few localities, the most notable being Girgenti, Sicily. Sulfur in native form occurs in volcanic rocks associated with fumarolic minerals (a *fumarole* is a volcanic vent). Native sulfur accounts for about half the world's supply. The rest is obtained as a by-product of the smelting of sulfur-containing ores, from pyrite (iron sulfide), and from "sour" natural gas. *Loc:* Sicily (Girgenti); Mexico; Japan; Chile; Texas; Louisiana—salt domes; Wyoming; Utah; Nevada; Hawaii.

Above: Diamond—Kimberley, South Africa. Opposite: Sulfur—Agrigento, Sicily (top); Graphite—Ceylon (bottom).

SULFIDES

Sulfides are minerals containing atoms of metals and sulfur; they include most of the minerals considered to be ores. Most sulfides are opaque. Some make colored streaks that are diagnostic in identification; many have a metallic luster. Usually classed with the sulfides are similar compounds containing selenium, tellurium, arsenic, and antimony.

Although sulfides of desirable metals, such as copper, may occur as disseminated flecks in a host rock, economically valuable concentrations can accumulate through a process known as *secondary enrichment*. In this process, surface waters dissolve the disseminated sulfide grains and carry their metallic content downward in the form of soluble sulfates. At a lower depth the sulfates react with fresh sulfides and redeposit their contained metals as *secondary sulfides*. Large concentrations of rich copper sulfides have formed in this way and are valuable ore deposits.

The chemical bonding in sulfides is similar in many respects to that in pure metals. Sulfides therefore exhibit many metallic properties, such as metallic luster and good electrical conductivity.

CHALCOCITE is one of the principal ores of copper, but only when it is concentrated by secondary enrichment in massive amounts or is present in high enough concentration as primary grains in a host rock. Crystals of chalcocite are rare, but have occurred at Cornwall, England, and at Bristol, Connecticut. *Loc:* U.S.S.R.; Chile; Peru; Mexico; South-West Africa (Tsumeb); Montana (Butte); Arizona; Nevada; Alaska.

46

*Above: Chalcocite—Bristol, Conn.
Opposite: Bornite—Butte, Mont. (l.); Chalcopyrite—
Concepcion del Oro, Mexico.*

BORNITE is a bronze-colored sulfide with a metallic luster, but fresh surfaces quickly tarnish due to oxidation in air. The thin film of surface oxide creates iridescence, hence the name "peacock ore." Bornite crystals are rare, but the mineral occurs in many deposits throughout the world, usually intergrown with chalcocite and chalcopyrite. It is an important ore of copper. *Loc:* England (Cornwall); Connecticut (Bristol); Montana (Butte); Austria; Italy; Madagascar; Chile; Peru; Bolivia; Mexico.

CHALCOPYRITE is brassy yellow in color but has a greenish-black streak. It resembles gold and pyrite but is harder than gold and softer than pyrite. Chalcopyrite is one of the most widespread copper minerals and an important source of copper. Crystals are common and usually resemble elongate tetrahedra. The mineral frequently tarnishes to a bright iridescence. Chalcopyrite forms in a wide variety of environments associated with many different minerals. *Loc:* Missouri (Joplin area); Colorado; Pennsylvania (French Creek); Mexico; Spain (Rio Tinto); Sweden (Falun); England (Cornwall); Japan; Chile; Peru; Bolivia; Scotland; South Australia (Wallaroo).

COVELLITE has a most distinctive color: a deep, metallic, indigo blue. The mineral is not abundant, but is found as a coating in many copper deposits. Crystals are rare and tend to be thin and platy. The mineral has good cleavage and tends to break into thin, flexible plates. *Loc:* Chile; Bolivia; Argentina; Peru; Sardinia; Saxony; Montana (Butte); Colorado; Wyoming; Utah; Alaska (Kennecott).

GALENA is easy to recognize because of its gray, metallic appearance and distinct cubic cleavage. Galena is also rather heavy, as befits the principal ore of lead. Galena crystals weighing hundreds of pounds are not uncommon; they tend to form as octahedra or cubes. Galena is also an important source of silver, which occurs in the sulfide as an impurity. The mineral occurs in veins, as well as in low-temperature deposits in limestone. There are hundreds of important localities. *Loc:* Oklahoma-Kansas-Missouri (Tri-State area where the three states are contiguous); Idaho; Utah; Colorado; Germany (Ems, Freiburg); England (Cornwall); Australia (Broken Hill); Austria; Rumania; France.

Above: Covellite—Butte, Mont. (top l.);
Galena—Treece, Kans. (top r.); Sphalerite—Joplin, Mo.
Opposite: Millerite—Antwerp, N.Y.

SPHALERITE is the chief ore of zinc. It is associated with galena almost everywhere either of the two minerals occurs. Sphalerite varies in hue from pale orange-yellow to deep red and black as its iron content increases, although the streak is always a pale yellow-brown. Sphalerite is virtually the only source of such minor metals as cadmium, indium, gallium, and thallium, which occur in the sphalerite as impurities. Crystals are common and usually very complex. Mode of origin and principal localities are the same as those for galena.

MILLERITE crystals are almost always needle-like and a bright, metallic yellow. Radiating tufts of crystals make attractive specimens. The mineral is, in general, too rare to be a major ore of nickel except at certain localities. It forms in low-temperature environments associated with other nickel minerals, sometimes in coal deposits, and rarely in volcanic rocks where it deposits from hot gases. *Loc:* Iowa (Keokuk); New York (Antwerp); Missouri; Wisconsin; Ontario (Sudbury); Wales; Germany (Siegen); Czechoslovakia.

PYRRHOTITE, a bronze-colored sulfide, is one of the few minerals attracted by a magnet. The higher the iron content of the pyrrhotite, the stronger the magnetism. Pyrrhotite is often closely associated with important ores of copper, nickel, and platinum, and is mined in huge quantities to recover the associated minerals. Enormous pyrrhotite crystals have been found in Mexico in recent years. Crystals are hexagonal, sometimes in thin plates, but these are comparatively rare. *Loc:* Brazil (Morro Velho); Maine; New York; Tennessee (Ducktown); Ontario (Sudbury); Germany (Freiburg, Schneeburg); Italy; Austria; Norway; Sweden; Mexico.

CINNABAR is the only important ore of mercury and is found in commercial quantities in only a few localities. The bright red color and scarlet streak are diagnostic in identification. Crystals are very rare and often twinned. The mineral is usually a primary, rather than a secondary sulfide. It occurs in low-temperature environments, in volcanic rocks. Only a few deposits produce much of the world's mercury supply. *Loc:* Spain (Almaden); California (New Almaden, New Idria); Nevada; Yugoslavia (Mt. Avala); China (Hunan Province); Mexico.

REALGAR is a fairly common mineral with a distinctive red color and resinous luster. It is almost always associated with the yellow arsenic sulfide, orpiment, in veins and around volcanos and hot springs. It tends to form in low-temperature environments. Crystals are sometimes elongate, but are usually short and chunky looking. Light causes eventual decomposition of realgar. Specimens are best stored in a dark place. *Loc:* Macedonia (Allchar); Washington; Nevada (Manhattan, Getchell Mine); Utah (Mercur); California (Boron); Japan; Switzerland; Rumania.

ORPIMENT derives its name from the Latin word *auripigmentum*, meaning "golden paint," and the mineral is indeed a bright yellow. It is found closely associated with realgar, though good crystals are not so common. It more commonly occurs as disseminated grains or in foliated or fibrous masses. Orpiment was widely used as a pigment and for removal of hair from animal skins. Localities are the same as for realgar.

Opposite: Pyrrhotite—Chihuahua, Mexico. Above: Cinnabar—Hunan, China (top l.); Orpiment— Yakutia, Siberia (top r.); Realgar—Transylvania, Rumania.

STIBNITE crystals are often curved and usually deeply striated. The mineral will melt in a match flame, and has excellent cleavage in one direction. Stibnite forms at relatively low temperatures and is usually found in veins or hot-spring deposits. It is the chief ore of antimony, and occurs throughout the world associated with such minerals as realgar, orpiment, cinnabar, and quartz. Magnificent crystal specimens come from Iyo, Shikoku, Japan, but the supply from this source is limited since the mines are exhausted. *Loc:* Rumania (Kisbanya, Felsobanya); California; Nevada (Manhattan); Greece; Italy (Pereta); China (Hunan Province); Mexico; Germany (Wolfsburg).

PYRITE is best known as "fool's gold," because of its brassy yellow color. It is the most common sulfide. Pyrite is much harder than gold and its streak is greenish-black. It occurs in rocks and deposits of all types, in both high- and low-temperature environments. Crystals are very common; they can be extremely complex or simple cubes. Pyrite is sometimes mined for its gold and copper content (present as impurities) and sometimes for iron or sulfur. There are literally thousands of localities throughout the world. Good crystals come from Italy (Elba); England (Cornwall); Peru; Bolivia; Mexico; Utah (Bingham); Pennsylvania (French Creek); Colorado (Leadville, Gilman).

MARCASITE and pyrite have the same composition, but differ in internal structure and external form. This condition is known as *polymorphism*. Crystals of marcasite are usually distinguishable from those of pyrite. Though it is not stable at high temperatures, marcasite is very widespread—commonly in crystals—in low-temperature environments. Marcasite sometimes forms rounded concretions, replaces the shell material in fossils, or crystallizes in veins with lead and zinc ores. "Cockscomb marcasite" forms crystal groups resembling the red appendage on the head of a rooster. *Loc:* Missouri-Oklahoma-Kansas (Tri-State area); Wisconsin; Mexico; France; England (Devonshire); Czechoslovakia.

ARSENOPYRITE is the principal source of arsenic, and may be distinguished from marcasite by its white, metallic color. It is a high-temperature mineral, and is frequently associated with gold in veins. When heated, arsenopyrite emits a garlic-like odor, a good test for the presence of arsenic. Crystals are common, and can be elongate or columnar, sometimes deeply striated. *Loc:* Bolivia (Llallagua); Switzerland (Valais); England (Devonshire); Mexico (Parral); Austria; Italy; Colorado; New Hampshire (Franconia); South Dakota (Homestake Mine); New Jersey (Franklin).

Opposite: Stibnite—Nagybanya, Rumania (top l.);
Pyrite—Butte, Mont. (top r.); Marcasite—Pitcher, Okla.
Above: Arsenopyrite—Chihuahua, Mexico.

SULFOSALTS

The name sulfosalt refers to early notions about mineral chemistry that have proved to be incorrect. Nonetheless the title for this mineral group is in such widespread use that it still serves to indicate a special type of sulfur-containing mineral which is not a sulfide. In general, sulfosalts contain both metals and semimetals (typically, arsenic or antimony) combined with sulfur. In ordinary sulfides, semimetals replace sulfur in the structure. In the sulfosalts, however, semimetals behave like true metals. There are only a few well-known sulfosalts, but among these are very highly prized specimen minerals.

PROUSTITE, with its bright red color and occasional transparency, is one of the most popular minerals among collectors. Crystals are not rare; some reach several inches in length. The mineral is light-sensitive, and will darken if exposed for long periods of time. Proustite is found in veins associated with other silver minerals. *Loc:* Czecho-slovakia (Jachymov); Chile (Chanarcillo); Ontario (Cobalt); Colorado; Idaho; Nevada (Silver City); Mexico.

PYRARGYRITE is more common than proustite but is a deeper red color and contains antimony rather than arsenic. Both proustite and pyrargyrite are called "ruby silver" because of their color and metallic content. Localities are the same as for proustite.

Above: Tetrahedrite—Isere, France (l.); Enargite—Butte, Mont. Opposite: Proustite—Chanarcillo, Chile.

TETRAHEDRITE and **TENNANTITE** have virtually identical structures. What differentiates them is the presence of antimony in tetrahedrite and arsenic in tennantite. There is, however, a complete range of possible compositions intermediate between the end-member compositions (no arsenic or no antimony), and the two minerals thus form ends of what is termed a **solid-solution series.** A solid solution is thus a structure in which one kind of atom can be partially or completely replaced by another. Tennantite is harder than tetrahedrite, but has a slightly lower specific gravity. These differences are very minute, and the two minerals resemble each other so strongly that it takes careful and detailed laboratory work to distinguish them. Both minerals occur commonly in tetrahedron-shaped crystals. *Loc:* Czechoslovakia; Germany; Austria; France; Algeria; England (Cornwall); Bolivia (Potosi); Montana (Butte); Idaho (Kellogg Mine); Utah (Bingham Canyon).

ENARGITE is a relatively rare mineral, whose large crystals are valued by collectors. The mineral is an important copper ore at Butte, Montana, where some of the best crystals have been found. Enargite has excellent cleavage (its name comes from a Greek word meaning "distinct," referring to the cleavage). *Loc:* Yugoslavia (Bor); Philippines (Luzon); Peru (Cerro de Pasco); Chile; Argentina.

OXIDES

Oxide minerals contain one or more metals combined with oxygen. If hydrogen is also present the mineral is termed a hydroxide. Groups within the oxide family are based on the metal-to-oxygen ratio. One oxide mineral—water—is a compound on which all life depends. (Water is indeed a mineral—it satisfies the definition of a mineral given earlier in this book.) Other oxides are important ore minerals (notably of iron and manganese); some oxides are used as abrasives, and others are used as gems.

Oxides tend to have simple structures and chemistries. Many oxides formed at high temperatures deep within the earth and these tend to be quite hard; other oxides form "rust-colored" blankets over ore bodies. Oxides and hydroxides of iron and manganese form much of the bright natural coloration of rock formations. The earliest known paints were oxides, and nodules of iron oxide are sometimes called "Indian paint pots."

CUPRITE is a common mineral in the oxidized zone of copper-bearing ore bodies, and in some places the mineral is an important ore itself. Crystals tend to be either simple cubes or felted masses of fine red needles. The fibrous variety, called **chalcotrichite,** makes lovely specimens. *Loc:* Arizona (Bisbee, Clifton, Morenci, Ray); New Mexico (Santa Rita); South-West Africa (Tsumeb); U.S.S.R. (Perm); France (Chessy); England (Cornwall); Australia (Broken Hill, NSW).

ZINCITE is a deep red-orange mineral known almost exclusively from a single deposit—Franklin, New Jersey. Here it is associated with calcite, willemite, and franklinite, an assemblage that occurs nowhere else on earth. Zincite usually forms red masses or grains, but occasional crystals are known. These are quite distinctive, having a flat base and a single hexagonal pyramid (like a six-sided party hat).

Above: Cuprite (var. chalcotrichite)—Morenci, Ariz. Opposite: Zincite—Franklin, N.J. (top); Rutile—Boiling Springs, N.C.

RUTILE can be colored black, red, or golden yellow. The mineral occurs in many different types of rocks. Quartz containing numerous fine, hair-like crystals is called "rutilated quartz" and is a popular gem material. Rutile is heavy and often concentrates in beach sands, where it can be mined for its titanium content. *Loc:* Brazil; Georgia (Graves Mountain); California; Arkansas (Magnet Cove); Switzerland; Norway.

CORUNDUM is used in diverse ways. Its great hardness (9 on the Mohs scale) makes it an excellent abrasive. Corundum occurs in virtually all colors and occasionally is transparent. When cut into gems, colored corundum is known as **sapphire;** blue is the best-known sapphire color, but the gem can be green, yellow, brown-orange, pink, or colorless. Deep red corundum has a special name: **ruby.** The finest rubies come from Burma, with lesser quality material from Thailand and Ceylon (though Ceylon sapphires are very fine). Corundum mixed with certain other minerals is called **emery,** an excellent abrasive. Synthetic corundum can be made in large quantities, and it finds use in watch bearings (the "jewels" in watches are synthetic corundum), abrasives, and jewelry. *Loc:* Burma; Ceylon; Thailand; North Carolina; Georgia; Massachusetts (Chester); U.S.S.R.; Switzerland; Madagascar; South Africa; Canada (Ontario).

CASSITERITE is the principal ore of tin. Crystals can be prismatic, needle-like, or rounded, and they are frequently twinned. Waterworn pebbles of cassiterite are termed "stream tin." The mineral commonly occurs in high-temperature veins, but it is present in commercial quantities in only a few places. *Loc:* Czechoslovakia (Schlaggenwald); England (Cornwall); Sumatra; Australia (New South Wales); South-West Africa; Bolivia (La Paz, Oruro); Mexico.

HEMATITE, a red, ocherous mineral is the most important ore of iron and among the most abundant minerals on the surface of the earth. Hematite in soils and as disseminated flakes and grains imparts the red color usually associated with "painted deserts" and landscape coloration. Crystals are common, and although these are black and metallic-looking they give a red streak (a diagnostic test). Large hematite iron-ore deposits make up the so-called "iron ranges" of Michigan and Wisconsin. **Specular hematite** consists of tiny, metallic flakes. "Kidney ore" is globular masses of hematite with a smooth fracture and sometimes a banded internal structure. *Loc:* England (Cumberland); Brazil (Minas Gerais); Italy (Elba); Switzerland (St. Gotthard); Michigan; Wisconsin; New York; Alabama.

CHRYSOBERYL is a hard, yellow or green mineral that rarely occurs in crystals. A variety containing fibrous inclusions yields gems known as **cat's-eye** or **cymophane.** Although other minerals may display "eyes" when cut, chrysoberyl is the true "cat's-eye" known in ancient times. A rare variety called **alexandrite** changes color (green to red) in different types of illumination. *Loc:* U.S.S.R. (Ural Mountains); Ceylon—cat's-eye; Czechoslovakia; Brazil; Madagascar; Maine (Oxford County); Connecticut (Haddam); New York.

Opposite: Corundum—Ontario, Canada (l.); Cassiterite—Schlaggenwald, Czechoslovakia (top r.); Hematite—Minas Gerais, Brazil. Above: Chrysoberyl—Espirito Santo, Brazil.

BAUXITE is the only ore of aluminum. It is, strictly speaking, a rock, since it is composed of a mixture of several aluminum hydroxides. It forms chiefly in warm and humid climates. *Loc:* France; Jamaica; Surinam; Arkansas; Georgia; Alabama.

SPINEL GROUP

The spinel group consists of a series of minerals that have similar structures and display extensive chemical variation. Most of these minerals tend to form octahedral crystals, but the colors vary from black to bright shades of red, blue, green, brown, and lavender. **Spinel** shows a great variety of color. "Ruby spinel" greatly resembles true ruby (corundum), so much that a large cut "ruby" in the Crown Jewels of England turned out to be a red spinel. **Gahnite** is a rare mineral that contains zinc. **Magnetite** is easy to identify because of its intense magnetism. This is an important ore of iron, with excellent crystals known from several localities. Magnetite, in small grains, is the black component of most beach sands. **Franklinite** is a zinc-rich magnetite from Franklin, New Jersey. **Chromite,** a spinel-group mineral, is the only ore of chromium. Other spinels contain manganese and magnesium, but are relatively rare minerals. *Loc:* Burma; Ceylon; Madagascar; Sweden (Kiruna); New Jersey (Franklin); New York; South Africa; Turkey; U.S.S.R.; Canada; Switzerland; many other localities worldwide.

60

*Above: Magnetite—Binnenthal, Switzerland (l.);
Franklinite—Franklin, N.J. Opposite: Bauxite—Ga. (top);
Manganite—Harz, Germany (l.); Goethite—Ishpeming, Mich.*

Hydroxides

MANGANITE is a black manganese hydroxide that occurs in veins and low-temperature manganese deposits. Crystals are usually well developed and can be quite large. The mineral is somewhat harder than the other manganese oxides it resembles, and it occurs in veins associated with these other oxides. Manganite is an ore of manganese. *Loc:* England (Cornwall); Germany (Ilfeld, Horhausen); Sweden; Nova Scotia (Picton County); Michigan; Virginia.

GOETHITE is a common mineral and forms in environments where iron-containing formations are exposed to weathering conditions. In large quantities goethite is an important ore of iron. The usual name for powdery or earthy, yellow-brown iron hydroxide is **limonite.** Limonite is amorphous, whereas goethite has a distinct crystalline structure. Fibrous specimens are common, and the mineral sometimes is found as inclusions in quartz. **Lepidocrocite** is identical in composition to goethite but has a different crystal structure. Localities are very numerous throughout the world. *Loc:* Cuba (Moa); Czechoslovakia (Pribram); France (Alsace); England (Cornwall); Michigan; Minnesota; Colorado; Utah (Pelican Point); Brazil (Minas Gerais).

HALIDES

Halides contain the *halogen* elements (fluorine, chlorine, bromine, iodine) and are of great economic importance. Most are soluble in water and are thus rarely exposed in humid climates. Others, such as halite (common salt), are abundant. The chemical bonding in halides is ionic (see p. 16) and not very strong. Thus, halides are soft and brittle.

The terms halide and halogen derive from the Greek word *hals*, meaning "salt" or "ocean." Large salt deposits originated by evaporation of salt lakes or small seas. Most of the water-soluble halides crystallize in the isometric system and display very simple crystal forms, such as the cube and octahedron.

HALITE—as table salt, or common salt—is the most familiar halide. Easily recognized by its taste, it is an essential food vitally needed by the human body. Table salt is a highly refined and purified form, but halite in less pure form is used to melt snow on roads and sidewalks in winter. Salt formations occur throughout the world, usually as dome-shaped structures, sometimes associated with sulfur and sulfates. The U.S., the world's largest salt producer, has mines in more than a dozen states. Good crystals—almost invariably simple cubes—are common and sometimes reach enormous size. Halite has hundreds of uses—in fertilizers, tanning of hides, and food preparation. In the chemical industry salt is used in the manufacture of sodium, chlorine, hydrochloric acid, and other compounds. *Loc:* New York; Louisiana; Texas; Michigan; Ohio; California (Searles Lake); Kansas; U.S.S.R.; China; England (Cheshire); Canada; Italy; West Germany; Poland (Wieliczka); Austria.

Above: Halite—Poland.
Opposite: Fluorite—Ill. (top);
Fluorite—Cave in Rock, Ill.

FLUORITE is a common mineral whose crystals are typically cubes or octahedra, though they also can be highly complex. Fluorite may be almost any color and sometimes the material is zoned or banded. Beautiful specimens are well known to mineral collectors. The mineral occurs in a wide variety of rocks and ore deposits. Some specimens fluoresce brightly (the term "fluorescence" derives from the phenomenon's appearance in the mineral fluorite). Fluorite is sometimes used as an ornamental material; large vases have been cut from banded purple material from England. It is also used as a flux in steel-making, in enameling cookware, preparing hydrofluoric acid, and in glass manufacture. The name "fluorite" comes from Latin; the word *fluere* means "to flow," and fluorite does indeed melt easily. **Chlorophane** is a variety that emits green light when heated. The cause of color in fluorite has been widely studied and is believed due to such factors as exposure to radioactivity and inclusions of rare earth elements. The color can be modified by heat, pressure, X-rays, and ultraviolet light. *Loc:* England (Derbyshire, Durham); Germany; Switzerland; Italy (Trentino); Norway; Mexico (Naica); New Hampshire (Westmoreland); Illinois (Rosiclare); Ohio; Missouri; Colorado; Connecticut (Trumbull); Virginia (Amelia Court House).

CARBONATES

In carbon-dioxide gas, which we exhale when we breathe, a carbon atom is joined to two oxygen atoms. In crystals, carbon surrounds itself with three oxygen atoms to form a *carbonate molecule,* or **radical** (from the Latin *radix* meaning root, or basic part). This radical occurs in a variety of compounds that therefore can be called carbonates. Acids release hydrogen, which is capable of breaking up the carbonate radical and releasing carbon-dioxide gas. This is the "fizz test" for identifying carbonates.

The carbonate radical has the form of an equilateral triangle, but this triangle can be oriented in various ways in mineral structures. One orientation leads to three-fold symmetry (since a triangle has three sides) that characterizes the **calcite group** and the **dolomite group** of minerals. When the triangle stands up on its base, it shows two-fold and mirror symmetry; this characterizes the **aragonite group,** which usually contains fairly large metal atoms in its structures. Other carbonate minerals display a variety of structures. Within the calcite group extensive chemical variation is possible, since the metals in these structures are all of similar size. Thus a crystal of calcite may have considerable iron in its structure (making it brown), or manganese (making it pink). Most carbonates are not "pure" compounds, but rather mixtures of several components.

CALCITE GROUP

*SIDERITE crystals usually are brown, but may be white or gray. Sometimes the brown color is only a surface layer and the mineral underneath is pale. Siderite is characteristic of low-temperature iron-ore deposits. It exhibits a variety of forms, and good crystals are common. *Loc:* Austria; Rumania (Baia Sprie); Switzerland; France (Isere); England (Cornwall); Greenland (Ivigtut); Canada (Mt. St. Hilaire); Brazil (Minas Gerais); Bolivia (Potosi); Colorado.

*Mineral belongs to group under which it appears.

✳CALCITE is the most abundant and common carbonate. A large part of the rock exposed at the surface of the earth is calcite in the form of limestone. Calcite is the dominant mineral in most **stalactite** and **stalagmite** cave formations. It occurs in all colors, due to finely admixed impurities, such as iron and manganese oxides. Crystals are very common and show an enormous diversity of forms, more than perhaps any other mineral. Twinning is also very common. Calcite fizzes in cold hydrochloric acid, a useful test since other carbonates do not react so readily. A variety of clear, colorless calcite known as **iceland spar** is used in optical devices and may occur in large masses. Calcite is often a cementing material in various types of rocks. Deposits that form around hot springs and geysers can be large and colorful. Calcite displays markedly a phenomenon called *double refraction,* which is the splitting of light into two beams polarized at right angles to each other. Writing seen through a calcite fragment thus appears to be doubled (see p. 32). *Loc:* England (Cumberland, Cornwall); Mexico (Guanajuato, Charcas); South-West Africa (Tsumeb); Iceland (Eskifjord); Michigan (Keeweenaw Peninsula); Missouri (Joplin); Illinois (Warsaw); New York; New Jersey (Paterson); thousands of other localities worldwide.

Above: Calcite—Missouri.
Opposite: Siderite—Auvergne, France.

RHODOCHROSITE is a favorite mineral among collectors because of its beautiful pink color. Rhodochrosite occurs in crystals up to several inches across and a deep rose-pink color. It is mined as a manganese ore in some localities. In one occurrence in Argentina, rhodochrosite makes up the carbonate mineral in a cave, resulting in pink stalactites and stalagmites that are prized by mineral collectors. The best crystal specimens come from Colorado and Mexico. Rhodochrosite occurs in many types of ore deposits. The name means "rose colored." *Loc:* Mexico (Cananea); Colorado; Montana (Butte); Rumania (Kapnik); Germany; England (Cornwall); Argentina (Catamarca Province).

SMITHSONITE occurs rarely in crystals, but rounded, banded masses in all colors are popular among collectors. The hardness and specific gravity are unusually high for a carbonate. Smithsonite forms in dry climates (honeycombed masses are called **dry-bone ore**) and is sometimes mined for its zinc content. Colors include white, gray, greenish, blue-green, blue, brown, and yellow. It is commonly found in veins associated with galena and sphalerite. It is named after James Smithson, founder of the Smithsonian Institution. *Loc:* South-West Africa (Tsumeb); France (Chessy); England (Cumberland); Australia (Broken Hill, NSW); Mexico (Boleo); New Mexico (Kelly Mine).

66   *Above: Smithsonite—Magdalena, N. Mex. Opposite: Rhodochrosite—Alma, Colo. (l.); Dolomite—Simplon Tunnel, Switzerland (r. top); Aragonite—Monroe County, Ind.*

DOLOMITE GROUP

✴**DOLOMITE** and **ANKERITE** are both members of the dolomite group which contains structures with carbonate radicals in combination with two metals: calcium, and either magnesium, iron, or manganese. Dolomite is of widespread occurrence, often mixed with calcite in large rock masses. It is believed that dolomite forms primarily due to alteration of limestone by solutions containing magnesium. Unusual saddle-shaped crystals are made up of small, misaligned blocks that produce curved crystal faces. Dolomite effervesces slowly in cold acids. Ankerite contains iron and is a common mineral. *Loc:* Switzerland; England; Mexico; Missouri (Tri-State area); New York; Brazil; Canada.

ARAGONITE GROUP

✴**ARAGONITE,** like calcite, fizzes in acid, but it does not have the good rhombic cleavage typical of the calcite group. Aragonite crystals are common and often appear as thin needles or tabular plates. Sometimes three crystals form a twin that resembles a short, hexagonal barrel. Aragonite is not so common as calcite because it is much less stable. The pearly layer in shells (such as mother-of-pearl) is aragonite. The mineral usually forms beds associated with gypsum or with hot-spring deposits. The name is from an occurrence at Molina de Aragon, Spain. *Loc:* Spain (Aragon); Austria; Italy (Sicily); England (Cumberland); Arizona; Colorado; New Mexico.

∗STRONTIANITE is a low-temperature mineral that occurs in a variety of geologic environments. It is the chief source of strontium, the element that produces red color in fireworks. It fizzes in acid, but is much denser than aragonite. Crystals are usually needle-like or prismatic; occasionally it occurs in curved, twisted crystals that resemble fishhooks. *Loc:* Germany (Westphalia); Scotland; Mexico (Coahuila); New York (Schoharie); New Mexico; California (Barstow); Texas; Louisiana.

∗CERUSSITE in glittering twinned crystal masses is one of the most attractive and desirable minerals. The brilliant adamantine luster and high specific gravity are distinguishing characteristics. Cerussite is occasionally an important ore of lead. The mineral forms as an alteration product of galena where weathering has progressed deeply in lead deposits. The best crystals come from Tsumeb, South-West Africa. Crystals are almost always twinned. The mineral forms at low temperatures, associated with a variety of bright-colored secondary minerals. *Loc:* South-West Africa (Tsumeb); Sardinia (Monteponi); Germany (Baden, Ems); Spain; France; Scotland (Leadhills); Rhodesia; Australia (Broken Hill, NSW); Pennsylvania; Colorado; Arizona; Nevada; Idaho; Utah; New Mexico.

MALACHITE is one of the best-known minerals among collectors. Almost any green fibrous mineral is likely to be labeled malachite in collections, but this is poor practice since other minerals have this appearance. Effervescence in acid proves that the mineral is a carbonate, however. Single crystals are rare. Dense banded malachite is mined as ore, but is attractive enough to be used as a gem material. Malachite forms almost anywhere copper ores have been reached by groundwater solutions and subsequently altered. *Loc:* Siberia; France (Chessy); Zaire; South-West Africa (Tsumeb); Australia; Arizona; Nevada; Utah.

AZURITE is named for its color, a distinctive deep blue. The mineral is less common than malachite, but it forms in similar environments and the two minerals are almost always associated with each other. Crystals can reach a length of 5 inches or more. The mineral can be an important copper ore when present in large quantities. Azurite crystals that are in the process of altering to malachite are known; they make interesting specimens. Localities are numerous. *Loc:* South-West Africa (Tsumeb); France (Chessy); Greece (Laurium); Australia (Broken Hill, NSW); Siberia; Arizona (Bisbee, Morenci); New Mexico.

68   *Strontianite—Oberdorf, Austria (top); Cerussite—Tsumeb, South-West Africa (middle l.); Azurite—Tsumeb, South-West Africa (middle r.); Malachite—Rhodesia.*

NITRATES

Nitrates are characterized by the nitrate radical, which consists of a nitrogen atom surrounded by three oxygen atoms in a planar triangle. This radical strongly resembles the carbonate radical, and carbonates and nitrates resemble each other structurally. The nitrates are so soluble, however, that their occurrence is limited to the driest parts of the earth; thus, they are not geologically important.

NITER and **SODA NITER** occur in desert areas, such as the incredibly dry Atacama Desert of Chile, where rain is almost unknown. The deposits are a bed up to a few feet in thickness, overlaid by sand and rock fragments. Crude soda niter is known as **caliche,** and forms by evaporation of groundwaters. The Chilean deposit is the only sizable deposit of nitrates and has dominated the world supply for many years. Nitrates are used in explosives and fertilizers. Crystals are very rare, and both niter and soda niter tend to occur as crusts or in massive beds. Small quantities of these minerals have been noted in California and Nevada, the driest desert regions of the U.S. *Loc:* Chile; Italy; Egypt; Iran; India; Spain; U.S.S.R.

70

BORATES

The boron atom is very small and tends to surround itself with three oxygen atoms to form a triangular borate radical. But the bonding is such that these radicals can link with additional oxygens to form sheets and chains. Melted borates tend to crystallize sluggishly, and if chilled quickly will form a glass (with no distinct crystalline structure). This effect is utilized in making a borax bead for certain mineral-testing procedures. Borates are·used widely in the manufacture of silica glass.

About 100 borate minerals are known, but only a few of them are common. **Kernite** occurs in million-ton quantities in the Mohave Desert, California. It was first discovered and described there in 1926 and immediately became the leading borax source. Like other borates, it swells and bubbles when heated in a flame. **Borax** crystals reach 6 inches or more in size. They are clear when mined but soon dehydrate to a form known as **tincalconite.** Borax, used as an antiseptic and washing agent, has been known and used for centuries. It is mined in Argentina, Chile, Bolivia, and California. **Colemanite** was the most important ore of boron until kernite's discovery. Crystals are usually distinct and well developed; good specimens come from California, the chief source of the mineral. **Ulexite** forms "cottonball" masses of fine crystals, which can reach 4 inches in diameter. It is also a source of borax. The mineral is known chiefly from California.

Opposite: Soda Niter—Iquique, Chile (top); Kernite—Calif. Above: Borax (altered to tincalconite)—Boron, Calif.

SULFATES and CHROMATES

The basic structural unit of the sulfate minerals is the sulfate radical. This consists of a sulfur atom surrounded by four oxygen atoms located at the corners of a tetrahedron. This tetrahedron is so tightly bonded that it retains its integrity even when the mineral is dissolved, and sulfate radicals thus can float about in solution; under suitable conditions they may recombine with metals to form new sulfate compounds. Most common sulfates are heavy. Some are soluble in water, some in acids, and some are insoluble even in strong acids. The insoluble sulfates tend to be pale colored or colorless, and translucent to transparent. There are many sulfates known, but only a few are common.

Chromates are among the most highly colored minerals. They are characterized by the chromate radical in which a chromium atom is surrounded by four oxygens in a tetrahedron (as in the sulfate radical). The only well-known chromate is a rare mineral, crocoite, which is sought for its brilliant red color.

Of the common sulfates, three are anhydrous (contain no water) and are grouped together (barite group). Other sulfates have varying amounts of water in their structures.

CROCOITE, though comparatively rare, is popular among collectors because of its bright red color. It occurs in the oxidized zones of lead deposits, where chromium has been introduced in the formation of the ores. Crystals are usually prismatic, and can reach several inches in length. *Loc:* U.S.S.R. (Beresovsk); Tasmania (Dundas); Rumania (Rezbanya); Brazil (Minas Gerais); Arizona; California.

BARITE GROUP

*BARITE crystals are very common. They are usually tabular, and can reach enormous sizes (over a foot in length). The habit can be simple or very complex. Barite color ranges from colorless to blue, yellow, reddish, and brown. The specific gravity (high) and cleavage (distinct to perfect) are both distinguishing characteristics. Sometimes barite crystals form penetrating aggregates resembling flowers; these are called "barite roses." Numerous localities have produced remarkably fine crystals. The chief use of barite is in the manufacture of drilling mud for oil wells. *Loc:* England (Cumberland, Derbyshire); Rumania (Felsobanya); Colorado (Sterling, Golden); Oklahoma (Norman)—for "roses"; South Dakota; New York (St. Lawrence Co.); Nova Scotia.

*CELESTITE crystals strongly resemble those of barite, but are slightly heavier. Celestite is, however, a much less common mineral than barite. It is frequently disseminated in limestone where it may form crystals in cavities. The mineral was first described from an occurrence of fibrous blue material at Bellwood, Pennsylvania. *Loc:* New York (Chittenango Falls); Ohio (Clay Center); Utah; Texas; Sicily (Girgenti); Egypt; Scotland; England (Bristol); Mexico; U.S.S.R.

Opposite: Crocoite—Dundas, Tasmania. Above:
Barite—Cumberland, England (l.); Celestite—Natural Bridge,
N.Y. (r. top); Barite—Cumberland, England.

73

✶ANGLESITE crystals tend to be more complex than those of barite or celestite. Anglesite forms as an alteration product of galena, and is usually found associated with that mineral or in the oxidized portion of lead deposits. Anglesite is a minor ore of lead, named for a locality in Anglesey, Wales. The mineral often fluoresces yellow in ultraviolet light. There are many known localities. *Loc:* Germany (Baden); Austria (Carinthia); France; Sardinia (Monteponi); England (Matlock); Wales (Anglesey); Australia (Broken Hill, NSW); Tasmania (Dundas); Mexico (Chihuahua); Pennsylvania (Chester Co.); Missouri; Utah; Arizona; Idaho.

ANHYDRITE crystals tend to be tabular, and are quite rare. The color ranges from colorless and white to gray, blue, and lilac. It forms large beds, associated with limestone gypsum and salt. It forms by direct evaporation of sea water or by dehydration of gypsum. Anhydrite also occurs in volcanic rocks and sometimes is associated with metalliferous veins. Localities are numerous. *Loc:* Austria (Salzburg); Switzerland (Bex); France; Germany (Stassfurt); Poland (Krakow); Japan (Ugo); Pakistan; New York; New Jersey (Paterson); New Mexico; Texas; Louisiana; Nova Scotia; Quebec.

GYPSUM is an abundant, widespread, and commercially significant mineral. Its chief use is in the production of plaster of Paris, and some is used in Portland cement. Gypsum has excellent cleavage and is quite soft (2 on the Mohs scale). **Satin spar** is a fibrous variety, and **selenite** is gypsum in crystalline form. Crystals are common and can reach lengths of several feet. A cave at Naica, Mexico, was found filled with gigantic gypsum crystals, leading to its fanciful name—"Cave of Swords." Beds of gypsum can be quite extensive and are usually interlayered with beds of salt and clay. Gypsum is the most common sulfate. Massive gypsum, called **alabaster,** is used as an ornamental stone. When sea water evaporates, minerals are precipitated in a sequence: gypsum, followed by anhydrite, then halite. Large gypsum deposits occur in salt lakes. The mineral occasionally forms in volcanic rocks, associated with sulfur. *Loc:* Sicily (Girgenti); Switzerland (Bex); France; Germany; Austria; Poland (Krakow); England (Oxford); Mexico (Naica); New York; Iowa; Michigan; New Mexico; Ohio; Canada.

ANTLERITE once was thought to be very rare, but in 1925 it was found in vast quantities at Chuquicamata, Chile, where it became the chief copper ore mined. In the U.S. antlerite is found in the Southwest. It is often confused with other copper minerals it much resembles, especially **brochantite.** Crystals of antlerite tend to be tabular, and are always deep green. *Loc:* Chile (Chuquicamata); Nevada; Arizona; Alaska; Mexico.

Opposite: Anglesite—Zeehan, Tasmania (top l.);
Gypsum—Naica, Chihuahua, Mexico (top r.); Anhydrite—Aussee,
Austria. Above: Antlerite—Chuquicamata, Chile.

PHOSPHATES, ARSENATES, VANADATES

These minerals are generally secondary in origin, forming through the alteration of other minerals. The basic radical in all three groups is a tetrahedron of oxygen atoms; in phosphates it is centrally occupied by a phosphorus atom, in the vanadates by a vanadium atom, and in the arsenates by arsenic. These radicals are almost the same size so there is considerable substitution of one for another in several groups of minerals.

The phosphate family is very large. but only a few members are common. Arsenates and vanadates are usually brightly colored, relatively soft (less than 6), and have high specific gravities. The phosphates tend to display a great diversity of structures but one group, the apatite group, contains several structurally related minerals.

VIVIANITE is generally blue or green in color and forms in low-temperature environments, such as in oxide nodules in fresh sediments. Crystals can be microscopic or as long as several feet. Vivianite is a rare mineral but the blue-green color and perfect cleavage are distinctive. *Loc:* New Jersey (Mullica Hill); Utah; Bolivia (Llallagua); England (Cornwall); Africa (Nigeria).

ERYTHRITE, sometimes called "cobalt bloom," is a common alteration product of cobalt arsenides and is a guide to the prospector looking for cobalt minerals. Its pink color and "dusty" appearance are distinctive; good crystals occasionally are found. The best crystals come from Morocco. *Loc:* Mexico; Morocco (Bou Azzer); Canada (Ontario); Germany (Schneeburg).

APATITE GROUP

✳**APATITE** is the most common phosphate mineral. It occurs in all colors, many types of rocks, and a wide variety of geologic environments. Apatite is a chief constituent of bone and teeth. It is found disseminated through rocks or concentrated in massive deposits; it is mined extensively as a source of fertilizer phosphate. *Loc:* Portugal (Panesqueira); Spain (Jumilla); Switzerland; U.S.S.R.; Canada; Mexico (Durango); Maine (Auburn); hundreds of occurrences worldwide.

✳**PYROMORPHITE** is structurally similar to apatite, with lead replacing calcium. If arsenic is present in place of phosphorus, the mineral is called **mimetite.** Pyromorphite forms in oxidized zones of lead deposits, and can be green, brown, or yellowish in color. Mimetite is red, orange, or yellow. *Loc:* Germany (Ems); Scotland (Leadhills); South-West Africa (Tsumeb); Mexico; Pennsylvania (Phoenixville).

✳**VANADINITE** contains vanadium, rather than phosphorus or arsenic. It forms in weathered lead deposits. Hexagonal crystals are common and have high luster and specific gravity. **Endlichite** is similar to vanadinite but contains considerable arsenic as well. Vanadinite is a source of vanadium and lead. *Loc:* Morocco (Mibladen); Arizona (Globe, Yuma Mine); California; Mexico (Villa Ahumada); Scotland (Leadhills).

Opposite: Erythrite—Bou Azzer, Morocco (l.); Vivianite—Poopo, Bolivia. Above: Pyromorphite—Ems, Germany (l.); Apatite—Panesqueira, Portugal (r. top); Vanadinite—Mibladen, Morocco.

WAVELLITE characteristically forms radiating nodules of fine crystals. The mineral is found in many localities, but is nowhere very abundant. Wavellite is commonly seen in tin veins, phosphorite deposits, and limonite ore beds. *Loc:* Arkansas (Hot Springs); Pennsylvania; Colorado; Bolivia (Llallagua); Czechoslovakia; Tasmania.

TURQUOISE crystals are extremely rare and always microscopic. Massive material, however, is abundant in many localities. This is fashioned into jewelry, and much of it is veined by material from its surrounding rock, or matrix, and is therefore called **turquoise matrix.** Much of the turquoise jewelry sold to tourists has been treated in various ways to deepen the color of the stone. *Loc:* Siberia; France (Montebras); Chile (Chuquicamata); Iran; New Mexico; Arizona; Virginia (Lynch Station)—crystals.

VARISCITE, like turquoise, is very rare in crystals but is found in massive form. Variscite also occurs in nodules, commonly intermixed with other phosphate minerals. Such nodules, when cut open, reveal an intricate pattern of mineralization. Variscite may be found in veins and in phosphatic sediments. *Loc:* Utah (Fairfield); Arkansas (Montgomery); Germany (Messbach); Austria.

Above: Turquoise—N. Mex. (l. top); Variscite—Fairfield, Utah (l. bottom); Wavellite—Hot Springs, Ark. Opposite: Adamite—Mapimi, Mexico (top); Torbernite—Aveyron, France (l. bottom); Autunite—Wash.

ADAMITE is not a common mineral, but well-crystallized specimens are popular among collectors. The color varies greatly, with pink and green caused by impurities of manganese and iron, respectively. Compact balls of radiating crystals are attractive specimens. It is occasionally found in zinc deposits. *Loc:* Greece (Laurium); Mexico (Mapimi); France (Cap Garonne); Nevada; Chile; South-West Africa (Tsumeb).

AUTUNITE occurs in spectacular crystal groups in several localities, formed due to the oxidation of uranium minerals. The yellow-green crystal plates are fairly distinctive and are easily recognized. **Torbernite** has the same structure as autunite, but contains copper instead of calcium. Both minerals usually occur together and strongly resemble each other. In many cases identification cannot be made with certainty, but a test for copper will be helpful. *Loc:* Zaire; Germany (Schneeburg); England (Cornwall); France; Portugal (Estremadura); Mexico (Moctezuma); Australia; North Carolina; South Dakota; Maine; Washington (Daybreak Mine).

TUNGSTATES, MOLYBDATES

Tungsten and molybdenum are fairly large ions, and the oxygen radicals they form tend to be somewhat flattened rather than perfect tetrahedra. Tungsten and molybdenum may substitute freely for each other in several families of minerals, resulting in numerous species of intermediate composition. Most of these have been given distinct names.

WOLFRAMITE is a black mineral that occurs in excellent crystals, sometimes of large size. When manganese replaces iron in its structure, the mineral is called **huebnerite** and is brown. Although relatively rare, wolframite is the chief ore of tungsten. The mineral forms at high temperatures and is generally associated with specific types of rocks (pegmatite and granite). *Loc:* Bolivia (Llallagua); Portugal (Panesqueira); Czechoslovakia (Zinnwald, Schlaggenwald); Colorado (Silverton); North Carolina; Peru (Cerro de Pasco).

SCHEELITE also is an ore of tungsten. Crystals are scarce but can reach large sizes (several inches across). Scheelite occurs in veins and tin deposits. It fluoresces bluish-white, which is an aid in prospecting. Synthetic scheelite has many important technological uses. *Loc:* Utah (Milford); Arizona; South Dakota; Korea; Czechoslovakia (Zinnwald); Germany; England (Cumberland); Switzerland; France.

WULFENITE is one of the most desirable mineral species among collectors, and occurs in magnificent crystal groups. Crystals are tetragonal, may be elongate or flattened but usually are simple prisms or pyramidal in shape. The color varies from yellow to orange and red, sometimes gray or white. Wulfenite is an important source of molybdenum, although molybdenite is the chief ore of this metal. Wulfenite is secondary in origin and forms in the oxidized portions of lead deposits. **Stolzite** has the same structure but contains tungsten instead of molybdenum. There are hundreds of occurrences, and many produce fine crystal specimens. *Loc:* Germany; Austria (Annaberg); Czechoslovakia (Pribram); Sardinia (Sarrabus); Morocco; Algeria; Australia (Broken Hill); Mexico (Mapimi, Sierra de Los Lamentos, Chihuahua); Zaire; South-West Africa (Tsumeb); Arizona (Red Cloud Mine, Yuma Mine, Hamburg Mine); New Mexico; Utah (Lucin district); Massachusetts (Loudville); Pennsylvania (Wheatley mines, Phoenixville).

Opposite: Scheelite—South Korea (top); Wolframite—Panesqueira, Portugal. Above: Wulfenite—Los Lamentos, Mexico (top); Wulfenite—Red Cloud Mine, Ariz.

SILICATES

Silicates make up about 90 percent of the earth's crust and represent one-fourth of all known mineral species. Four elements—oxygen, silicon, aluminum, and iron—constitute more than 85 percent of the outer shell of the earth. These elements are also the primary ingredients in silicate minerals, and so silicates are justly called the "rock-forming minerals."

For many years it was thought that silicates, when dissolved, form siliceous acids. The rocks deposited from such solutions would therefore have to be "acid" rocks, and would be high in silicon oxide (silica). Rocks low in silica were called "basic" rocks. We now know that these acids do not exist in nature, but the terms acid and base, as applied to rocks, are still widely used.

The internal structures of silicates, as revealed by X-ray diffraction techniques, are based on variations in arrangements of silicon tetrahedra. This radical, consisting of a silicon atom surrounded by four oxygen atoms, is the basic structural unit in all silicates. Linkage schemes of these tetrahedra provide an effective way of classifying silicates.

In **nesosilicates,** silicon tetrahedra are isolated from one another, but are linked through bonds to cations in the mineral structures. In **sorosilicates,** two SiO_4 tetrahedra are joined at one corner, forming a "bow-tie" shaped group. If several tetrahedra link at corners to form a closed loop we have rings of 3, 4, 6, or more tetrahedra. Structures built on these groupings are called **cyclosilicates.** Silicon tetrahedra may also link together to form chains characteristic of the **inosilicates.** The chains may be single or double strands of tetrahedra, and some are very complex. Many rock-forming minerals belong to this group.

Phyllosilicates are sheet-structure minerals in which silicon tetrahedra link at corners to form layers of unrestricted lateral extent. Bonding is strong within the sheets, but weak between them, resulting in platy crystals and excellent cleavage parallel to the layers. Many families of minerals are phyllosilicates, since considerable variation in the composition and arrangement of the tetrahedral sheets is possible.

The **tectosilicates** make up about 75 percent of the rocky crust of the earth. In these minerals tetrahedra are linked at all corners to form three-dimensional arrays. Great variation in the structural scheme of such linkages is possible, and many of the common minerals are tectosilicates.

Structural variety is predictable on the basis of atomic sizes, charge, and bonding characteristics. Actual determination of the structures of silicates makes it possible to arrange this huge family in a meaningful way.

SILICATE TYPES

NESOSILICATE

SOROSILICATE

All Use the
Silicon Tetrahedron

CYCLOSILICATE

CYCLOSILICATE

INOSILICATE

INOSILICATE

PHYLLOSILICATE STACKING

TECTOSILICATE LINKAGE

*All silicates contain a fundamental unit called
the silicon tetrahedron. Differences in linking and stacking of
tetrahedra result in different silicate types.
Silicate families are characterized by isolated tetrahedra, double
tetrahedra, chains, rings, sheets, or networks in 3 dimensions.
Many silicates contain more than 1 of these arrangements.*

Nesosilicates

WILLEMITE is a hexagonal mineral that occurs at only a few localities, the most notable being Franklin, New Jersey. Here, however, it is abundant enough to be a zinc ore. The mineral is best known for its striking green fluorescence in ultraviolet light. *Loc:* Belgium; Algeria; Congo; Rhodesia; Greenland; New Mexico; Colorado; New Jersey (Franklin).

ZIRCON is an "accessory mineral," that is, one that occurs in a wide variety of rocks in small amounts. Gem zircons in many colors are produced by heat treatment. The mineral is the chief source of zirconium, a metal used to make *refractories* (substances with extremely high melting points) and shielding material for nuclear reactors. Crystals are common and usually are simple in form. *Loc:* Norway; U.S.S.R.; Sweden—variety **cyrtolite;** Italy; Madagascar; Ceylon; Maine; Massachusetts; New York; Colorado.

DATOLITE is a widespread mineral that occurs typically in volcanic rocks, such as basalt. The pale green or white color, glassy appearance, and complex crystals are distinctive. Massive varieties tend to be granular or crumbly. Crystals are usually wedge-shaped, and can reach 3 inches or more in size. *Loc:* New Jersey (Paterson); Massachusetts (Westfield); Michigan (Keeweenaw Peninsula); Canada (Ontario); Mexico (Guanajuato); Italy (Trentino).

OLIVINE actually refers to a group of minerals that have the same structure but differ chemically. **Fayalite** is an iron silicate, and **forsterite** is magnesium silicate. The iron and magnesium in the olivine structure occupy the same positions, and a range of possible compositions exists between the magnesium and iron "end-members." Olivines are important rock-forming minerals and are the first minerals to form in a mass of cooling molten rock deep within the earth. The gem variety is called **peridot.** *Loc:* Egypt (St. John's Island); Burma; Brazil (Minas Gerais); Vermont.

TOPAZ crystals are common and can reach enormous size (over 100 pounds). Its chief use is as a gem, and as such it is frequently referred to as "precious topaz" or, if the color is a rich golden hue, "imperial topaz." Many varieties of quartz are erroneously called topaz. Gem colors of true topaz are (including colorless) pink, pale blue, brown, pale yellow, and golden yellow. *Loc:* Brazil (Minas Gerais); U.S.S.R.; Utah (Thomas Mts.); New Hampshire; Texas; Colorado.

TITANITE, also commonly called **sphene,** typically occurs in distinctive wedge-shaped crystals. In some places it is mined as an ore of titanium. Gem varieties have high dispersion and high luster. *Loc:* Brazil (Minas Gerais); Switzerland; Canada (Ontario); Mexico (Baja California); New York (Rossie).

Opposite: Willemite—Franklin, N.J. (top l.);
Zircon—Tigerville, S.C. (bottom l.); Datolite—Great Notch,
N.J. Above: Olivine—Hawaii (top l.); Titanite—
Minas Gerais, Brazil (bottom l.); Topaz—Mursinka, Siberia.

ANDALUSITE is a common mineral, occasionally mined when present in large quantities. It is used as a refractory, but clear, transparent varieties can be cut as gems. The name comes from Andalusia, Spain. **Chiastolite** is a variety showing characteristic diamond-shaped carbonaceous inclusions. **Viridine** is a green variety. Andalusite occurs primarily in metamorphic rocks. *Loc:* U.S.S.R.; Austria; Germany; France; Spain (Andalusia); Australia (Mt. Howden); Brazil (Minas Gerais); Massachusetts; Maine (Standish).

KYANITE is also an accessory mineral in metamorphic rocks. It is occasionally found in large crystals of gem quality but these are rare. The mineral displays three different hardnesses on different crystal faces, a remarkable demonstration of the low symmetry of its structure. Kyanite, andalusite, and the mineral **sillimanite** all have the same composition, but each has a unique structure. *Loc:* Brazil; U.S.S.R.; Italy; Switzerland (Pizzo Forno); France (Morbihan); Connecticut (Litchfield); North Carolina.

STAUROLITE occurs in twins that are so characteristic that they are diagnostic of the species. Several twin laws exist in staurolite; right-angle penetration twins are given the fanciful name "fairy crosses." *Loc:* Switzerland (Ticino); France (Morbihan); Maine (Windham); Virginia; Georgia (Fannin Co.); North Carolina.

Above: Uvarovite—Outokumpu, Finland (l.); Almandine —Spruce Pine, N.C. Opposite: Kyanite—N.C. (l.); Andalusite— Mass. (r. top); Staurolite—Fannin County, Ga.

GARNET GROUP

Superb crystal specimens and exquisite gems are characteristic of the six minerals comprising this group. The garnets are an excellent example of minerals with the same basic structure but with different atoms occupying equivalent structural sites. **Pyrope, almandine,** and **spessartine** all contain aluminum, silicon, and oxygen, plus another principal cation (magnesium, iron, or manganese respectively). Similarly, **uvarovite, grossular,** and **andradite** all contain calcium, oxygen, and silicon, and are differentiated according to content of chromium, aluminum, or iron respectively. Most garnets actually contain several metals in addition to the ones that determine the species. This leads to wide variation in chemistry and also in color, form, and occurrence for these minerals. All the garnets are isometric and quite hard. Localities number in the thousands. Crystals range enormously in size. All the garnets have gem varieties although those of almandine are most common. **Rhodolite** is intermediate in composition between pyrope and almandine; **essonite** is a variety of grossular, **demantoid** is a green andradite, and **melanite** is black andradite that contains titanium.

Sorosilicates

HEMIMORPHITE, formerly called **calamine,** is common in secondary zones of lead and zinc deposits. Crystals are common and often form spectacular radiating groups. Hemimorphite is an ore of zinc; its name alludes to the low crystal symmetry that results in crystals with different arrangements of faces on opposite ends. *Loc:* Siberia (Nerchinsk); Rumania; Austria (Bleiberg); Sardinia (Monteponi); England (Cumberland); Mexico (Chihuahua); New Jersey (Franklin); Missouri; Colorado.

IDOCRASE is also known as **vesuvianite,** because the mineral was noted on the slopes of Mt. Vesuvius, Italy. It contains both sorosilicate groups and isolated silicon tetrahedra. The mineral forms in a wide variety of geologic environments and in many types of rocks. Crystals are common, and both color and morphology are extremely diverse. A green, massive variety resembling jade is called **californite.** *Loc:* Italy (Ala, Vesuvius); Mexico (Morelos); U.S.S.R.; Norway; Maine (Sanford); New Jersey (Franklin); Arkansas (Magnet Cove).

PREHNITE occurs in a variety of colors; crystals are rare. The mineral most commonly lines cavities in volcanic rocks such as basalt, and is usually some shade of green. Other minerals typically crystallize on top of the prehnite, yielding specimens desirable to collectors. *Loc:* Nova Scotia; New Jersey (Paterson); Massachusetts; Michigan.

Above: Idocrase—Wilui River, U.S.S.R. (top l.); Prehnite—Paterson, N.J. (top r.); Epidote—Untersulzbachtal, Austria (bottom l.); Zoisite (tanzanite)— Tanzania. Opposite: Hemimorphite—Mapimi, Mexico.

EPIDOTE GROUP

Both sorosilicate clusters and isolated silicon tetrahedra exist in the epidote structure. Some members of the group are monoclinic, while others are orthorhombic; these structures are related by twinning. Extensive chemical substitution is possible among the epidote minerals, giving rise to a variety of species. **Epidote** is usually brown or green due to the presence of iron. Crystals can be very large and spectacular. *Loc:* Austria (Untersulzbachtal); Alaska (Prince of Wales Island); California; Mexico.

Clinozoisite has the epidote structure but contains aluminum rather than iron. **Piemontite** is a pink mineral that contains manganese instead of aluminum or iron. **Allanite** is an epidote-like mineral containing rare earth elements, and sometimes uranium and thorium (making it slightly radioactive). Clinozoisite crystals tend to be small and colorless, piemontite crystals are very rare, and allanite is usually massive, granular, and dark colored (brown or black). **Zoisite** is the orthorhombic equivalent of clinozoisite. The two minerals strongly resemble each other, but zoisite is less common. Blue gem-quality zoisite crystals from Tanzania have been cut and marketed as **tanzanite,** a name without mineralogical significance. **Thulite** is a rose-red zoisite that contains manganese.

Cyclosilicates

All the cyclosilicates are characterized by rings of SiO_4 tetrahedra; several types of rings are known. The simplest consists of three tetrahedra linked to form a triangle with the composition Si_3O_9. A more complex ring contains four tetrahedra with a square configuration, having the formula Si_4O_{12}. Both of these types of rings are relatively rare. Most of the important cyclosilicate minerals contain rings with six silicon tetrahedra and composition Si_6O_{18}. The hexagonal symmetry of such rings often is reflected in the symmetry of minerals in which they occur. A few rare minerals contain very complex rings with double layers and intricate interconnections.

AXINITE has a complex structure containing Si_4O_{12} rings as well as other atomic groups. This leads to very low symmetry, and crystals tend to be thin and sharp-edged. Axinite is usually brown or green. *Loc:* Switzerland; England; France (Bourg d'Oisans); Japan (Kyushu); Mexico; Nevada; New Jersey.

BERYL is one of the best-known cyclosilicates, and occurs throughout the world in granitic rocks and pegmatites. Crystals are common. All colors are used as gems; the major color varieties are **emerald** (green), **aquamarine** (blue), **goshenite** (colorless), **morganite** (pink), and **heliodor** (gold). Beryl is the chief ore of beryllium and crystals can weigh several tons. Emerald is one of the most highly valued of all gems. *Loc:* Brazil (Minas Gerais); Colombia—emerald; Madagascar; Connecticut; North Carolina—emerald; California; Colorado; South Dakota; Canada; India.

CHRYSOCOLLA is an amorphous, compact, blue mineral found where copper minerals have been attacked by groundwater solutions. The composition and color are variable. Crystals are not known, and the mineral occurs in many localities throughout the world. Chrysocolla is often intimately mixed with quartz, and the mixture is hard enough to be cut as a gem. *Loc:* Arizona (Bisbee, Clifton, Morenci); New Mexico; England (Cornwall); Chile.

TOURMALINE GROUP

Tourmaline is actually a group name for minerals having the same structure but differing widely in occurrence, form, and composition. Individual species have distinct names: **elbaite** contains lithium and is a colored gem species; **schorl** is black and opaque and contains iron; **dravite** is a brown magnesium-bearing species. Color varieties include **achroite** (colorless), **rubellite** (pink), **siberite** (purplish-red), **indicolite** (blue), and **verdelite** (green). Absence of a center of symmetry makes the tourmalines intensely piezoelectric and pyroelectric. The structure contains Si_6O_{18} rings as well as BO_3 groups like those in borates. The complex structure leads to great variation in composition. *Loc:* Brazil (Minas Gerais); Italy (Elba); Madagascar; U.S.S.R.; California (Pala); New York (Pierrepont); Connecticut (Haddam Neck).

Opposite: Axinite—Bourg d'Oisans, France (l.); Beryl—Kleine Spitzkopje, South-West Africa. Above: Elbaite—Minas Gerais, Brazil (l.); Chrysocolla—Ariz.

Inosilicates

Inosilicates are characterized by the presence of chains of SiO₄ tetrahedra extending through their structures. These chains can be simple oxygen-linked strings, or they can be complex double chains. In both cases the chains are bonded laterally to cations of various types, leading to different mineral species. Simple chains are found in the **pyroxenes** and **pyroxenoids;** double-chain structures are characteristic of the **amphiboles.** These groups are similar in appearance, but can best be distinguished by cleavage. The pyroxenes break at angles of about 90 degrees, while the amphiboles cleave at angles of about 56 degrees. The amphiboles also contain water and yield vapor when heated in a closed glass tube; the pyroxenes, in contrast, are anhydrous. Pyroxenes commonly form stout, chunky, or sometimes prismatic crystals; the amphiboles tend to be fibrous or very elongate. Pyroxenes alter to amphiboles under certain conditions of temperature and pressure. Included among the inosilicates are many minerals and varieties. Most are important rock-forming minerals.

PYROXENES

Pyroxenes include several groups of minerals, all either monoclinic or orthorhombic. **Enstatite** and **hypersthene** are both orthorhombic (both have monoclinic counterparts). They occur throughout the world in high-temperature rocks. Crystals are rare, and both minerals are usually brown or black in color. *Loc:* New York (Brewster), North Carolina (Webster); Norway (Telemark).

✽**DIOPSIDE, HEDENBERGITE,** and **AUGITE** are all monoclinic and are among the most common pyroxenes. Diopside is rich in magnesium, hedenbergite contains iron, and augite has an intermediate composition. Crystals are prismatic or short and stubby. Hedenbergite is black; augite tends to be dark colored, but diopside can be pale green and even transparent varieties are known. Diopside occurs abundantly in limestones altered by heat and chemical action, usually associated with idocrase and grossular. *Loc:* New York (De Kalb); Italy (Piedmont); Switzerland (Ala); Sweden (Nordmark)—hedenbergite; Ontario (Renfrew)—augite.

✽**SPODUMENE, JADEITE,** and **AEGIRINE** are monoclinic pyroxenes with similar structures. Spodumene occurs in several gem varieties, of which the pink are called **kunzite** and the green **hiddenite.** Crystals tend to be flattened, coarse, and deeply etched. Some 40-feet long have come from South Dakota's Etta Mine. *Loc:* South Dakota; North Carolina (Stony Point, Hiddenite); California (Pala); Brazil (Minas Gerais); Madagascar. Jadeite is rarely in isolated crystals, but usually forms masses of tiny interlocked fibers called **jade.** Jade is very tough material used for carvings and jewelry; at times it has even been used for anvils. The term jade includes both jadeite (a pyroxene) and **nephrite** (an amphibole). Jade is best known from China, Burma, Alaska, and Central America. Aegirine crystals are fibrous or elongate, and either brown or green. **Acmite** is a rare species in rocks rich in sodium.

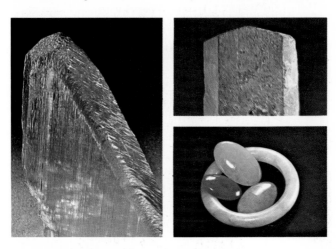

Opposite: Diopside—Piedmont, Italy. Above:
Spodumene (kunzite)—Calif. (l.); Enstatite—Bamle, Norway
(r. top); Jadeite—various localities.

PYROXENOIDS

Pyroxenoids are similar to the pyroxenes, except the chains are not made up of single SiO_4 tetrahedra. Rather, the pyroxenoid chains are composed of Si_2O_7 (sorosilicate) groups alternating with single tetrahedra. The repeating unit along such chains may also vary (one, two, or three groups of Si_2O_7), giving rise to a variety of related structures.

✱**WOLLASTONITE** is a white, fibrous mineral which occurs chiefly in impure limestones altered by heat. Other crystal forms are rare. The mineral is sometimes mined as the raw material for making ceramics. *Loc:* New York (Willsboro); California (Crestmore); Rumania (Cziklova); Mexico (Chiapas).

✱**PECTOLITE** typically occurs in balls of radiating, needle-like crystals. Large, prismatic crystals are rare. Massive pectolite is also known. The normal occurrence is in volcanic rocks altered by solutions. *Loc:* New Jersey (Paterson); Arkansas (Magnet Cove); Italy; Scotland; England.

✱**RHODONITE** crystals strongly resemble those of many pyroxenes and tend to be chunky. Massive rhodonite may contain inclusions of black manganese oxides, making it an attractive gem material. Rhodonite is pink or red due to manganese, and is sometimes confused with rhodochrosite (which is much softer). **Bustamite** and **fowlerite** are varieties. *Loc:* Australia (New South Wales); Sweden (Langban); New Jersey (Franklin).

Above: Pectolite—Paterson, N.J. Opposite: Wollastonite—Ikedoken, Japan (top l.); Rhodonite—Franklin, N.J. (top r.); Tremolite—St. Lawrence County, N.Y. (bottom l.); Hornblende—Ontario, Canada.

AMPHIBOLES

Amphiboles are characterized by double chains of silicon tetrahedra. The chemistry of this group is extremely complex; some amphiboles are monoclinic and others are orthorhombic. Orthorhombic amphiboles are usually classed in the **anthophyllite** series; their monoclinic analogs are placed in the **cummingtonite** series. Anthophyllite is rare in isolated crystals and usually forms brown, fibrous masses. The monoclinic equivalent, cummingtonite, usually contains more iron. *Loc:* Norway (Kongsberg); Greenland; North Carolina; Pennsylvania; Massachusetts (Cummington).

✳**TREMOLITE** and **ACTINOLITE** usually form prismatic or fibrous crystals. The color varies from white in tremolite through pale or deep green in actinolite. Fibrous varieties are sometimes matted and bear the descriptive nicknames **mountain leather** and **mountain cork.** Compact, fibrous masses can be very hard, and this material is called **nephrite** (a jade mineral). Some fibrous amphiboles are used as asbestos. *Loc:* Italy (Piedmont); Switzerland; China; New Zealand; Mexico; Wyoming; New York (De Kalb); Vermont (Chester).

✳**HORNBLENDE** is a very common amphibole. Crystals are usually dark green or black. The chemistry is very complex, so material with a variety of compositions is called hornblende, though many varieties have been given names. Localities are numerous.

Phyllosilicates

The structural scheme of the phyllosilicates is that of sheets of SiO_4 tetrahedra. The name itself comes from the Greek word *phyllon,* meaning "leaf," and the phyllosilicates have a characteristic platy habit and cleavage. Individual plates may be flexible or elastic, tend to be relatively soft, and have a low specific gravity. The bonding within the sheets tends to be strong, while that between the sheets is weak. The perfect cleavage along these planes reflects the planes of weakness in the structure. Most phyllosilicates contain water, and the position of the water and various metal atoms is important to the properties of the various phyllosilicates. Individual structural layers have hexagonal symmetry, but stacking of these layers produces an offset resulting in monoclinic symmetry for most of the phyllosilicate minerals.

APOPHYLLITE resembles the cyclosilicates in structure, because its structural layers contain rings of four SiO_4 tetrahedra linked together. The perfect cleavage in the mineral is characteristic of the phyllosilicates. Crystals are tetragonal, often perfect, and sometimes quite large. Apophyllite occurs in volcanic rocks as a secondary mineral. *Loc:* Oregon; Washington; New Jersey (Paterson); India (Poona); Nova Scotia; Greenland; Brazil (Rio Grande do Sul).

SERPENTINES are common minerals that form as an alteration product of various other silicates, especially pyroxenes. The most common species are **antigorite** (platy) and **chrysotile** (fibrous). Chrysotile is the most widespread and important asbestos mineral. It is mined in enormous quantities throughout the world. Asbestos is incombustible and fibrous, properties that allow it to be woven into fireproof cloth. Serpentine is common and occasionally forms masses of huge size (**serpentinite**, a rock, is massive antigorite). *Loc:* Serpentine: worldwide. Asbestos: Canada (Asbestos; Thetford); U.S.S.R.; Arizona; Rhodesia.

TALC crystals are rare, but massive material is quarried in many parts of the U.S. The extreme softness of this mineral (1 on the Mohs scale) makes it useful as talcum powder, but the mineral also has many industrial uses. A massive form called **soapstone** is used in sinks and table tops, and in carving. **Pyrophyllite** is a soft mineral, similar to talc, which occurs in pearly or greasy masses. *Loc:* North Carolina; Georgia; Texas; California; Vermont.

CLAY MINERALS

Clay minerals are all characterized by microscopic crystal size. Most "clay" specimens actually consist of mixtures of several minerals. Individual crystals are so small that they cannot be seen with normal microscopes. All the clays are hydrous aluminum silicates, usually containing some magnesium, iron, and sodium or calcium. **Kaolinite** is the most common clay and usually forms as an alteration product of other silicates. Similar species include **dickite, nacrite, halloysite,** and **montmorillonite.** *Loc:* Every soil.

Opposite: Talc and Soapstone—North Carolina (top); Apophyllite—Paterson, N.J. Above: Asbestos (Chrysotile)—Canada.

MICAS

Micas are minerals characterized by perfect cleavage and flexibility of individual cleavage sheets. Crystals are monoclinic, but may appear hexagonal. The internal structure is so similar in the mica minerals that several species may crystallize together in parallel position.

✳MUSCOVITE is usually pale-colored or colorless. It is widespread and abundant in many types of rocks, especially granites and pegmatites. Large crystals are called "books" and can be several feet across. **Sericite** is a fine-grained form. Large sheets of muscovite are used in electrical apparatus as insulators, in furnace doors, and at times as window panes. Some Canadian crystals have measured over 8 feet across. *Loc:* Canada; Sweden; Ireland; England; U.S.S.R.; India.

✳PHLOGOPITE is usually yellow-brown or green in color, though transparent in thin sheets. The mineral occurs abundantly in limestones in many localities. **Biotite** is very similar but is black and contains much iron; thin sheets are opaque. Biotite is an important constituent of many types of rocks. *Loc:* Numerous locations worldwide.

✳LEPIDOLITE contains lithium and is usually yellow or pink. It is comparatively rare, and is associated with other lithium-bearing minerals. **Margarite** is similar to the micas, but has a slightly different structure. Its brittle nature is characteristic of the group of so-called "brittle micas" to which it belongs.

*Above: Biotite—Wakefield, Quebec (l.); Muscovite—
Minas Gerais, Brazil. Opposite: Model of tectosilicate crystal
structure (top l.); Lepidolite—Minas Gerais, Brazil (top r.);
Clinochlore—Tilly Foster Mine, Brewster, N.Y.*

CHLORITES

Chlorite minerals are similar species that are difficult to differentiate without detailed tests. The principal minerals in the group are **clinochlore, penninite,** and **prochlorite. Kaemmererite** is a red chromium-bearing species. All the chlorites are monoclinic. Crystals are small and rare. Chlorite is nonetheless an important and widespread mineral group, and chlorites occur in a variety of rock types. The green color and nonelastic sheets are characteristic (except for kaemmererite). Some rocks are composed entirely of chlorite, or else are colored green by finely divided chlorite contained in them. *Loc:* New York (Tilly Foster Mine); Pennsylvania (West Chester); Texas; Austria; Switzerland; Turkey—kaemmererite.

Tectosilicates

Tectosilicates have framework structures in which SiO_4 tetrahedra are linked at all corners. Tectosilicate structures are strongly bonded and tend not to have specific planes of strong or weak bonds. Most minerals in this group tend to be pale-colored or white, insoluble in acids, low in specific gravity, and relatively hard.

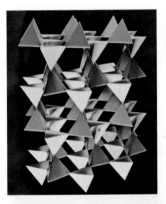

SILICA GROUP

Silica is SiO_2. This simple oxide is capable of crystallizing in nine distinct forms. The most common and familiar of these is the mineral **quartz**. The mineral occurs in virtually all colors (five varieties have specific gem names) and in a huge variety of forms. Colorless quartz **(rock crystal)** is used in the electronic industry. Quartz makes up most of the common beach sands, and also the rocks sandstone and quartzite. Crystals can be many feet long in pegmatites. Quartz often contains inclusions of other minerals, such as rutile and tourmaline. **Aventurine** is quartz containing flakes of mica.

Fine-grained quartz is called **cryptocrystalline** when the grains are microscopic. Many varieties are popular gem materials, such as **carnelian** (red), **chrysoprase** (apple-green), **agate** (banded or with moss-like inclusions), **chalcedony** (fibrous and often banded), **onyx** and **sardonyx** (banded in black and white), **bloodstone** (green chalcedony with red spots), **flint** and **chert** (dark, massive nodules), **prase** (dull green), and **jasper** (usually dull red or brown).

Quartz is widespread and occurs in a variety of geologic environments. Localities are too numerous to mention. Uses of quartz include

Above: Dendritic Agate (l. top);
Agate (l. bottom); Quartz (Amethyst). Opposite:
Jasper (top); Precious Opal.

concrete, abrasives, glass, sandpaper, scouring soaps, and scientific instruments.

When quartz is heated above 573 degrees Centigrade, its structure rearranges itself into a high-temperature form called **tridymite.** Above 1470 degrees tridymite breaks down and reforms as **cristobalite,** the stable form of SiO_2 above this temperature. **Stishovite** and **coesite** are formed only at high pressures.

Opal is hydrated silica with a variable water content. Opal is less hard than cryptocrystalline quartz and is almost always translucent or opaque. Some varieties (called **precious opal**) display brilliant internal colors in the form of flecks or sheets of "fire." **Fire opal** is orange or red in body color, and may or may not have internal "fire." **Hyalite** is clear, colorless opal which often fluoresces brilliant green. **Geyserite** is opal deposited around hot springs and geysers, and **diatomite** (diatomaceous earth) is a rock made of the silica shells of diatoms—tiny animals that live in the oceans.

Lechatelierite is fused silica glass that sometimes forms when lightning strikes a beach, or in the heat generated by a meteorite impact.

FELDSPARS

Feldspars are so common in the crust of the earth that the average composition of the entire crust is very close to that of a typical feldspar. Feldspars form both monoclinic and triclinic crystals which show good cleavage. In feldspars and other tectosilicates, aluminum joins with oxygen atoms to form tetrahedra that are almost exactly the same size as silicon tetrahedra. Aluminum and silicon are therefore thought to substitute for each other in tetrahedral positions in these structures.

There are three major feldspar groups, all with essentially the same structures but with differing chemical composition. They are potassium feldspars, sodium-calcium feldspars, and barium feldspars. Feldspar is used in making porcelain and glass.

POTASSIUM FELDSPARS

Orthoclase occurs in many types of rocks, and displays cleavage angles of almost 90 degrees. Crystals tend to be stubby and are often twinned in characteristic ways. **Sanidine** is a potassium feldspar found in volcanic rocks, and **adularia** is typical of low-temperature veins. Good crystals of adularia come from Switzerland.

Microcline is triclinic and is nearly always twinned. **Graphic granite** is a rock containing quartz and microcline grown together in a complex way. Microcline forms some of the largest-known mineral crystals (one from Russia weighed over 2,000 tons). Other notable localities include Colorado (Pike's Peak), Virginia, and North Carolina. **Amazonite** (amazonstone) is a blue or green variety frequently used as a gem material.

SODIUM-CALCIUM FELDSPARS

Sodium-calcium feldspars, also called the **plagioclase feldspars,** form a complete series of minerals in which sodium and calcium replace each other structurally. The series is split up (arbitrarily) into six minerals, each of which covers a particular range of sodium/calcium ratios. The six members are: **albite** (all sodium), **oligoclase, andesine, labradorite, bytownite,** and **anorthite** (the last being all calcium). The properties of all members of the group are essentially the same, and the minerals can best be distinguished by chemical or optical tests. Twinning is common, especially in albite.

Albite is found in various types of rocks, especially those that are coarsely crystalline. A variety known as **cleavelandite** has a platy habit and is common in the U.S. Albite with a bluish sheen is called **moonstone.** Crystals from Switzerland are exceptionally fine.

Oligoclase sometimes has a bluish color, and occurs in North

Labradorite (showing Schiller effect)—Labrador (top l.); Orthoclase—Colorado (top r.); Adularia—St. Gotthard, Switzerland (bottom l.); Albite—Amelia, Va.

Carolina and New York. Reddish inclusions produce the variety **sun-stone.** Andesine and bytownite are less common feldspars. Andesine is found in volcanic rocks, and occasionally bytownite that can be faceted occurs in reddish masses.

Labradorite contains inclusions of other feldspars that create a blue or golden sheen, called *"Schiller."* This feature makes labradorite an attractive gemstone. Certain types of rocks contain labradorite as a primary constituent, and these are slabbed and used as facing material in buildings. Good material comes from New York, Labrador, and Norway.

Anorthite is quite rare but forms good crystals in volcanic rocks at Mt. Vesuvius, Italy, and Franklin, New Jersey.

BARIUM FELDSPARS

Barium feldspars are structurally similar to the potassium feldspars. **Hyalophane** is a barium-bearing adularia whose crystals resemble those of adularia. It is known from Switzerland (Valais), Sweden (Orebro), and New Jersey (Franklin). **Celsian** is similar to anorthite, with barium replacing calcium. It is monoclinic and occurs in Sweden (Vermland) and Switzerland (Candoglia).

FELDSPATHOIDS

Feldspathoids are similar to the feldspars in composition. Their chemistries are, however, marked by the presence of unusual anions, such as chlorine and sulfur, that are rarely found in silicates. These anions are able to fit into large open spaces in the framework structures and create odd colors in these minerals.

NEPHELINE is hexagonal, has a greasy luster in massive varieties, and strongly resembles quartz. Pure masses are used in glass manufacture. **Cancrinite** is similar to nepheline in occurrence. *Loc:* Norway; South Africa; Canada (Ontario).

SODALITE is a relatively rare mineral, but is well known as a gem material because of its rich blue color. Related minerals include **nosean** and **hauyne.** Crystals are very rare, but occur in lavas at Vesuvius, Italy. **Lazurite,** a member of the sodalite group, is also very rare but the massive material is the Biblical stone, **lapis lazuli.** Ground-up lazurite was used as the paint pigment, **ultramarine.** Lazurite is always associated with pyrite and other silicates. Fine material comes from Iran and Chile.

LEUCITE forms characteristic isometric crystals similar to those of some garnets. Leucite crystals always have a dull luster and are enclosed in matrix rock. The name is from the Greek *leukos,* meaning "white." *Loc:* Italy (Mt. Vesuvius, Mt. Albani, Capo di Bove); Arkansas (Magnet Cove).

Above: Sodalite—Ontario, Canada (l.); Leucite—Vesuvius, Italy. Opposite: Lazurite (lapis lazuli)—Chile (top l.); Cancrinite— Litchfield, Maine (top r.); Wernerite—Ontario, Canada.

SCAPOLITE GROUP

Scapolites are relatively common minerals with compositions similar to those of feldspars. Although they are tectosilicates, scapolites contain ring-like groups of four SiO_4 tetrahedra. In color they appear colorless, white, blue, gray, green, yellow, pink, violet, brown, and orange. Crystals are usually coarse and sometimes large.

Marialite is a sodium-bearing scapolite; **meionite** contains calcium rather than sodium, and **wernerite** is a name used to designate all intermediate compositions. *Loc:* Madagascar; Massachusetts (Bolton); New York; Canada (Ontario); Norway; Sweden; U.S.S.R. (Siberia).

ZEOLITES

Zeolites are related silicates that frequently occur together. All are tectosilicates that contain primarily sodium, calcium, and potassium. Most zeolites are white or pale-colored, have low specific gravities (less than 2.5), and are relatively soft (3–5). When heated, zeolites boil and fuse as water is driven out of their structures. This behavior gives rise to the name zeolite, which comes from Greek words meaning "boiling stone." There are about 50 minerals in the zeolite group, but other nonzeolites are almost always associated with them.

Natural and artificial zeolites are used widely as water softeners. Zeolites typically occur in altered volcanic rocks and form at low temperatures. **Zeolite associates** are minerals commonly found associated with zeolites, and include calcite, prehnite, and pectolite.

✳**NATROLITE** is orthorhombic and usually forms long, needle-like crystals. Similar-appearing species are **mesolite** and **scolecite,** both of which are monoclinic. The three minerals can be differentiated by optical tests. *Loc:* Brazil; New Jersey (Bergen Hill, Paterson); New Zealand.

✳CHABAZITE is a hexagonal mineral that nearly always forms rhomb-shaped crystals. The color varies from white to pink, yellow, and red. A similar species, **gmelinite,** usually displays more complex crystals. *Loc:* New Jersey; Nova Scotia.

✳HEULANDITE is monoclinic and crystals have a characteristic "coffin shape." Cleavage is perfect in one direction, and cleaved surfaces have a marked pearly luster. *Loc:* Iceland; New Jersey.

✳ANALCIME resembles leucite, but analcime crystals have a glassy luster and grow freely into open spaces in a host rock. Analcime crystals several inches across are known. *Loc:* New Jersey; Michigan; Washington; Quebec (Mt. St. Hilaire); Nova Scotia.

✳STILBITE is monoclinic and its typical habit is fan-shaped aggregates which resemble wheat sheaves. *Loc:* New Jersey; Oregon; Washington; Nova Scotia; India; Scotland.

Opposite: Natrolite—West Paterson, N.J. (top l.);
Analcime—Frombach, Italian Tirol (top r.); Chabazite—
Paterson, N.J. Above: Stilbite—Prospect Park Quarry, N.J.

SYNTHETIC MINERALS

Man has always been curious about the way minerals grow in nature. Little of this information can come from direct observation, since minerals often form in environments of high temperature and pressure that are inaccessible to man. But by growing crystals in the laboratory scientists can determine the conditions in which they form most easily. It can be inferred that similar conditions account for the formation of crystals in geologic environments.

Mineral synthesis is now a routine part of mineralogical investigation. Knowledge of crystal growth processes has application in other fields and has made possible such devices as lasers and portable radios and television sets. Controlled crystal growth has also revolutionized the field of gemmology, since many types of gem materials have been synthesized in the laboratory.

The crystals grown commercially often reach stupendous sizes. Quartz crystals weighing almost five pounds are commonplace, and these are dwarfed by the half-ton sodium iodide crystals grown for the electronics industry.

Big crystals grow from small crystals both in the laboratory and in nature. Small crystals, called *seeds,* are produced first and these form the nuclei for larger crystals. Many different techniques for growing crystals are in current use. The most familiar are growth from vapor, from a melt, and from solution.

Vapor growth is the formation of a crystal directly from a vapor or gas. Snowflakes—crystals of ice—are the best-known examples. The lacy, branching forms of snowflakes are a result of very rapid crystal growth, which characterizes growth from a vapor.

The solidification of an ingot of molten metal is a good example of melt growth. Many types of synthetic gem materials (ruby, sapphire, spinel) and optical materials (calcite, fluorite) are grown from melts. Ice is a crystalline material normally grown from molten ice (water).

Growth from solution is a commonplace process both in nature and in the laboratory. Material dissolves in a solvent (typically water) at a high temperature until the resulting solution is *saturated*—that is, it can dissolve no more material at that temperature. Since less material is permitted in the solution at low temperatures, when the saturated solution cools the excess dissolved matter is ejected. If this process takes place slowly the ejected solid can build up very gradually on a small crystal of the same substance placed in the solution. This accretion on a seed results in the growth of the seed into a larger crystal. Growth continues as long as material is ejected by the solution. Many minerals form this way in veins, precipitating from *hydrothermal* (literally, "hot water") solutions. Long periods of crystal growth can lead to single crystals of enormous size. The largest known natural crystals weigh hundreds of tons.

In all three types of crystal growth a fundamental change of state occurs. In a molten material, for example, the atoms are moving about rapidly (they move even more rapidly in a vapor). If the temperature is high enough to keep the substance molten, the atoms move so rapidly that they cannot stick together effectively, but rather slip and slide over one another. This results in the fluid behavior of liquids and vapors.

As the temperature is lowered, the atoms slow down, and eventually a temperature is reached where atomic clusters can form that do not immediately break up again. Soon all the atoms in the liquid have settled into a fixed position with respect to their neighbors. Such an arrangement is, in fact, a periodic and regular array of atoms—a crystal. The difference between a solid and a liquid or vapor is the long range orderliness of atoms in the solid. The atoms in a liquid are moving about too freely to retain any long-range periodicity. Thus all solids are, by definition, crystalline.

As a crystal grows, new material is added in such a way that the orderliness of the atomic arrangement is preserved and extended. The slower the crystal grows, the more likely it is that the atoms added to it can find their correct positions before being covered by new material. Thus, slowly grown crystals tend to be more perfect and transparent (as in the case of gem crystals) than rapidly grown crystals. Nature has almost infinite patience, and natural crystals may take thousands of years to form. Such crystals tend to display the beauty and perfection so prized by man throughout history.

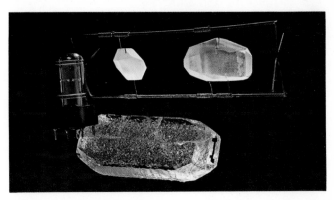

Quartz is produced in the laboratory in much
the same way it grows in nature. Crystals grow from "seeds"
held in a rack at high temperature and pressure.

5
Gems and Gem Minerals

Minerals that have ornamental value are gems. Gemstones include both minerals and organic materials (such as coral and pearl), but the latter are not very durable. A gemstone that is cut and set in a mounting suitable for wearing is called a *jewel*. Jewelry is thus, strictly speaking, ornamental and functional; the term does not apply to uncut gemstones or unmounted gems.

Many minerals are used as gemstones. The chief characteristics of a gem material are: hardness, durability, rarity, color, transparency (in faceted gems), and beauty. A material may be cut as a gem in spite of deficiencies in one or more of these qualities. For example, many minerals are normally opaque or translucent but occasional transparent pieces are found. When cut, these minerals may be quite lovely but too rare to become widely known and desired. Some minerals are too soft to make durable, wearable gems, while others are so common that they are seldom cut commercially. Some minerals occur in a wide range of colors (such as elbaite and beryl), and all the color varieties are potential gems when sufficiently transparent. Other gem materials are always the same color (malachite). A few minerals rank high in all gem characteristics. These have been called the "precious" gems (all others being "semiprecious"), but these terms are scientifically meaningless. The most highly valued gems are emerald, diamond, ruby, and sapphire. Other rare (and very costly) gem materials are alexandrite (a variety of chrysoberyl) and topaz in a deep, golden-yellow color called "imperial topaz."

Today a gemmologist must be a technical specialist, because of the proliferation of man-made synthetic and imitation materials. Ruby was synthesized as early as 1880, and in recent years emerald, sapphire (all colors), spinel (all colors), diamond (in very small sizes), and many other gem minerals have been successfully manufactured in large quantities. These man-made gems are not imitations or fakes. They are chemically and structurally identical with the natural materials. In some cases (as with star sapphire and ruby), the synthetics generally look far better than most natural stones.

Imitation gems, on the other hand, are materials that have properties

Gems have been prized by man since   **111**
ancient times. Minerals in transparent form or displaying
exceptional color are most popular.

mimicking those of another, more valuable gem material. Thus, yttrium aluminum garnet (YAG) has brilliance and sparkle similar to that of a diamond, and gems made of this garnet are "imitation diamonds." The industrial diamonds made by General Electric, however, are true diamonds with hardness and other properties equivalent to natural stones. The terms "synthetic" and "man-made" apply to laboratory-grown counterparts of natural minerals, while "artificial" and "imitation" apply to materials with some properties similar to those of natural gemstones, but not with the same chemical composition and atomic structure.

POPULAR GEM VARIETIES

BERYL Varieties are colorless, pink, blue, blue-green, green, and yellow. **Emerald** and **aquamarine** are well-known gems; other colors are less prominent.

TOURMALINE Elbaite is the colored variety cut as a gem. The typical colors are green (various shades), pink, and blue; color-zoned crystals make attractive gems. Shades of brown and yellow are scarce.

CHRYSOBERYL When inclusions are present, this material cuts cat's-eye stones. A variety that shows a color change (red in incandescent light, green in daylight) is called **alexandrite,** and is one of the costliest gems.

DIAMOND occurs in many colors, but these are relatively rare. The largest known diamond, when found, weighed 1⅓ pounds.

CORUNDUM Second in hardness only to diamond; the blood-red variety is called **ruby,** while **sapphire** is corundum of any other color. Large rubies are the rarest of gems and the most valuable. Star sapphire and star ruby contain inclusions of another mineral oriented in parallel bundles of fibers. Light striking these produces oriented reflections that form a star in cut stones.

OPAL Common opal is a drab gray, green, or buff-colored material. Some types of opal show brilliant displays of color, called *fire*, concentrated in dots, flecks, and sheets in the material. This is **precious opal.** **Fire opal** does not display fire, but rather is a red or orange and is translucent to transparent. Fine material comes from Mexico, but the best precious opal comes from Australia.

112   *Clockwise from top left: Tourmaline, Spinel, Chrysoberyl, Topaz, "canary" Diamond, "star of Asia" Star Sapphire, Precious Opal, color varieties of Beryl.*

SPINEL occurs in a wide variety of colors. One variety, called ruby spinel, has the color of very fine ruby and is sometimes mistaken for the more valuable corundum gem.

TOPAZ is common in pale colors, but the yellow-orange "imperial" variety is highly prized. Blue, colorless, and pink stones have much less value. Topaz crystals can weigh hundreds of pounds.

ZIRCON, after heating, yields a wide range of colors. The blue and colorless varieties are the most common and inexpensive.

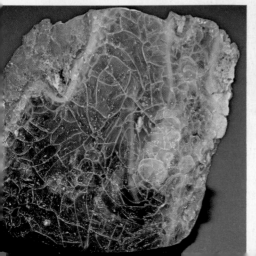

SPODUMENE is found in several gem varieties. **Kunzite** is pale pink to deep rose red in color; **hiddenite** is a rare green variety, originally found in North Carolina.

GARNET All six species of garnet are cut as gems. **Almandine** and **spessartine** are the most common garnet gems, varying in color from red to orange. Brilliant stones of green **grossular** and orange **andradite** are known from Africa, and the deep green **uvarovite** makes a rare gem. **Pyrope** is a wine-red color. Two gem varieties are **rhodolite,** which is the color of fine amethyst, and **demantoid,** deep green in color and one of the rarest of all gems.

PERIDOT is the mineral **olivine,** a common rock-forming mineral. Its rare gem-quality crystals yield lovely gems.

TURQUOISE, a blue copper mineral, was known in ancient times. High-quality material is rare, and the dying of inferior material is a common deceptive practice.

MOONSTONE is a variety of albite that displays a bluish or silvery sheen. Sometimes faceted gems are cut from colorless albite that also displays the blue sheen in certain orientations.

QUARTZ occurs in many colors; popular gem varietiés include **amethyst** (purple), **citrine** (yellow), rose, smoky, and colorless. Citrine is often sold as a variety of topaz, but this is simply misrepresentation. Amethyst is the most valuable quartz gem, and in deep colors it can command high prices.

114

Above: Kunzite (l.), Zircon (r. top),
Spessartine Garnet. Opposite: Amethyst (l.), Peridot
—olivine crystal (r. top), Coral.

ORGANIC GEM MATERIALS

AMBER is the fossilized remains of tree sap. It is often fashioned into beads and pendants, although it is really too soft to have much value in jewelry. Sometimes amber contains the remains of ancient insects that were trapped in the sap before it hardened.

PEARL is one of the most valued of gems. A pearl is the product of a living oyster, an attempt by the animal to protect itself from abrasion by a tiny foreign particle in its soft tissues. The oyster coats such a particle with successive layers of aragonite, until the particle is enclosed. The layers of protective coating form a pearl. *Mother-of-pearl* is the iridescent shell of certain marine animals, such as abalone.

IVORY is the tooth material (tusks) of elephants, although the teeth of certain whales, boars, and walrus also provide ivory. This material is usually carved in intricate and ornate designs.

CORAL is the hard material secreted by tiny marine organisms. Coral is usually white or drab gray, but it occasionally is lustrous black or a delicate shade of pink. The colored varieties have ornamental value and are carved, or even worn in the form of natural branching pieces.

⑥ Rocks and Rock Formations

Rocks, the most familiar materials on earth, are made up of minerals. Whereas a mineral is a homogeneous substance with specific structure and composition, a rock may contain several minerals in varying proportions. Any specific rock name is therefore flexible and includes material showing a range of composition and texture.

Rocks are classified according to their history and the minerals they contain. The study of rocks, called *petrology*, tells us a great deal about the conditions in which rocks formed and thus about the history of our planet. Two aspects of petrology are *petrography*, the study of the physical characteristics of rocks, and *petrogenesis*, the study of rock origins. Rock nomenclature is very complex and detailed because of the variable nature of rock compositions and the lack of distinct lines of difference between rocks with similar chemistry and texture. Classification is therefore based on broad generalities. There are three broad categories of rocks: igneous, sedimentary, and metamorphic.

Igneous rocks form as the result of cooling of molten material. Mineral crystals form as the temperature drops below their melting points. Exactly which minerals form depends on the starting composition of the molten mass (called *magma*) and the rate of cooling. Slow cooling results in the formation of large crystals, while rapid cooling produces tiny crystals or sometimes even a glass in which distinct crystals have not had a chance to form. The way the minerals in a rock grow together is a feature called rock *texture*. Igneous rocks can cool slowly deep within the earth. This produces large crystals and characteristic coarse textures. When igneous rocks are forced into cooler regions near the surface of the earth they cool more quickly and develop fine-grained textures or even chill to a glass. Igneous rocks can thus be classified according to grain size, though what is considered fine or coarse grain may sometimes be a matter of judgment; no grains are visible in glasses. Rocks containing exactly the same minerals, even in the same proportions, have different names depending on the size of the crystals present. This enables geologists to differentiate rocks according to their cooling history.

Rocks not only tell an interesting story of birth and growth of the earth, but are responsible for scenic wonders, such as the falls of the Yellowstone River.

Sedimentary rocks form at the surface of the earth due to *erosion,* the action of wind, water, and ice which causes rocks to break up and scatter their components. Marine animals build shells out of carbonate minerals and silica. When the animals die their shells settle to the bottom and build up thick deposits that later are compressed and become rocks. Particles carried by streams and the wind may also build up into layered deposits. Rocks formed in this way are called *sedimentary* because they are composed of sediments. Sediments can be particles of mineral matter (such as sand, pebbles, or clay) or chemicals precipitated by organic or inorganic action. The former types are called *mechanical* or *clastic* (fragmentary) sedimentary rocks and the latter are termed *chemical* sedimentary rocks. Both types make up a substantial portion of the earth's crust. Since sedimentary rocks form by the settling of particles (the word "sediment" comes from the Latin *sedimentum* meaning "settling") they often display a layered structure. This is the most characteristic feature of such rocks.

Metamorphic rocks form by the alteration of other kinds of rocks. Such alteration can come about through intense heat and/or pressure, perhaps accompanied by the introduction of new material. Metamorphic rocks are classified according to their degree of alteration and the nature of the rocks from which they formed. Metamorphic processes usually occur in periods of deformation of the earth's crust, as during mountain-building episodes. Rocks altered over a wide area due to large-scale forces are termed *regional metamorphic rocks;* those affected by local action are called *contact metamorphic rocks.*

The chief characteristic of metamorphic rocks is a change in texture. In many cases the grain size of the rock increases. Sometimes pervasive pressure on a rock over a long period of time forces individual mineral grains into alignment, producing a texture of *lineation.* An extreme case of this is called *foliation,* a laminated structure of minerals in extreme parallelism.

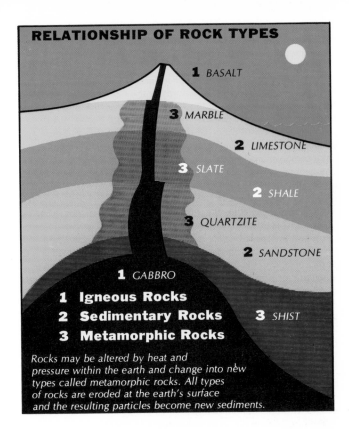

RELATIONSHIP OF ROCK TYPES

1 BASALT
3 MARBLE
2 LIMESTONE
3 SLATE
2 SHALE
3 QUARTZITE
2 SANDSTONE
1 GABBRO

1 Igneous Rocks
2 Sedimentary Rocks
3 Metamorphic Rocks

3 SHIST

Rocks may be altered by heat and pressure within the earth and change into new types called metamorphic rocks. All types of rocks are eroded at the earth's surface and the resulting particles become new sediments.

The earth is constantly changing and rocks are continually being melted, deformed, squeezed, and abraded. Since the earth is a closed system (nothing added and nothing removed), the chemical elements it contains are repeatedly mixed and separated by geologic processes. We may think of all rock types as forming a cycle in which some types are gradually changed into others. Igneous and metamorphic rocks form from melting and squeezing of sedimentary rocks, and in turn are worn away to become new sediments. All of these processes are taking place today, dramatically confirming the principle of *uniformitarianism* proposed by James Hutton in 1795. The present is indeed the key to the past.

History of a portion of the earth's crust can be learned from study of formations such as these pronounced folds located east of Sterling Hill, N.J.

IGNEOUS ROCKS

Igneous rocks form in conditions of high temperature and sometimes high pressure as well. They are therefore composed almost exclusively of silicates, and chiefly those with high melting points. **Intrusive** igneous rocks cool and crystallize deep within the earth or amid other types of rocks at shallower depths. Their textures are generally coarse due to slow cooling. **Extrusive** rocks form by the rapid cooling of molten material ejected onto the earth's surface. Extrusive rocks are therefore fine grained or glassy, due to very rapid cooling.

This overall classification of igneous rocks is based on texture and cooling history rather than composition. Therefore, every intrusive rock has a compositionally identical counterpart among the extrusive rocks. The general appearance of an igneous rock is largely determined by the type of minerals it contains. Amphiboles, pyroxenes, micas, and olivine are frequently dark colored, and rocks rich in them are called *mafic, basic,* or *melanocratic* (from the Greek word *melanos,* meaning "black"). These dark minerals are collectively termed *ferromagnesians* because they tend to be rich in iron and magnesium. Rocks containing abundant quartz and feldspar are light colored, and termed *felsic, acidic,* or *leucocratic* (from the Greek word *leukos,* meaning "white"). *Ultrabasic* or *ultramafic* rocks are very dark and usually consist wholly of olivine, with perhaps some pyroxene.

Igneous Formations

A **formation** is a rock mass that can be described as a unit. It may consist of one rock type or several types that are considered together for geologic reasons. Formations may also be recognized because they are somehow unique and stand out from surrounding rocks. Intrusive igneous rock formations are known in all parts of the earth.

Batholiths are very large intrusions, sometimes extending over 100,000 square miles. They cut across pre-existing rock layers and are thus called *discordant plutons;* a pluton is any igneous rock formed below the surface of the earth. The Greek word *bathos* means "deep," and batholiths increase in size downward. Their slow cooling leads to uniform and moderate grain size; the chief rock in most cooled batholiths is granite. Batholiths form from magma chambers that feed most volcanic activity, and they are associated with many types of ore deposits. They often form the cores of mountain ranges, such as the Sierra Nevada of California.

A **laccolith** is an intrusion formed when magma is forced into overlying rocks, pushing them up into a dome shape. The base of a laccolith is usually parallel to the rock beds below it, but the top is in the

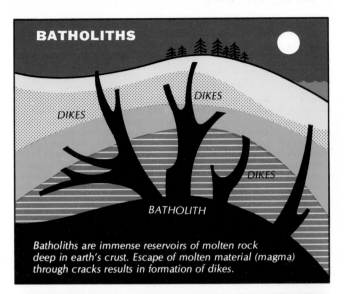

BATHOLITHS

DIKES

DIKES

DIKES

BATHOLITH

Batholiths are immense reservoirs of molten rock deep in earth's crust. Escape of molten material (magma) through cracks results in formation of dikes.

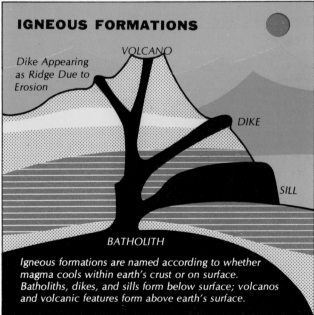

IGNEOUS FORMATIONS

VOLCANO

Dike Appearing as Ridge Due to Erosion

DIKE

SILL

BATHOLITH

Igneous formations are named according to whether magma cools within earth's crust or on surface. Batholiths, dikes, and sills form below surface; volcanos and volcanic features form above earth's surface.

form of a "blister." If both the top and bottom of an intrusion are parallel to structures in the intruded rocks, and the intrusion is more than ten times longer than it is thick, the intrusion is called a **sill.** The Palisades Sill near New York City is a well-known example.

Dikes are tabular rock masses that form when magma is injected into other rocks along fissures and cracks, and hence at an angle

Spectacular violence of volcanic eruptions testifies to dynamic forces at work on—and within—our planet. This is 1968 eruption of Cerro Negro, in Nicaragua.

to any layered structure that may be present in the intruded rocks. Dikes therefore stand out conspicuously when exposed. They are sometimes present in an area in large numbers, giving rise to "dike swarms." The heat accompanying intrusion bakes the surrounding rocks and may produce a variety of new minerals. Dikes cool rapidly and are thus composed of fine-grained rocks, such as dolerite. Dikes may be as wide as 500 feet, and as much as 50 miles long.

Volcanos

Volcanos are landforms built of molten material that has spewed out onto the earth's surface. Such molten rock is called *lava*. Volcanos may be no larger than small hills, or thousands of feet high. All have a characteristic cone shape. Some well-known mountains are actually volcanos. Examples are Mt. Fuji (Japan), Mt. Lassen (California), Mt. Hood (Oregon), Mt. Etna and Mt. Vesuvius (Italy), and Paricutin (Mexico). The Hawaiian Islands are all immense volcanos whose summits rise above the ocean, and these volcanos are still quite active.

Extrusive rocks are associated with volcanic activity. Lava may emerge in quiet flows that cover thousands of square miles of land; the Deccan Plateau of India and the Columbia Plateau of the American Northwest are examples. Volcanic activity may also be quite violent, as is the case with eruptions. These are spectacular events in which steam and lava are thrown into the air. The eruption of Krakatoa (in Indonesia) in 1883 obliterated two huge volcanic cones and the noise was heard 3,000 miles away. Dust created in the explosion fell throughout the world for two years afterward.

Shield lava cones are volcanic cones built of quiet effusions of lava; *spatter cones* and *cinder cones* are built of fragments ejected more energetically. *Volcanic bombs* are masses of lava that have been thrown into the air and hardened in an aerodynamic shape.

Pyroclastic rocks include all deposits of fragments thrown out by volcanos and deposited on the ground. Fragments may be large *(blocks)*, inch-sized or smaller *(cinders)*, or very fine particles *(ash)*. Ash that has been consolidated into rock is called *tuff*. Some types of volcanos are made of lava only, while others are composed of various types of material and are called *composite cones*.

Lavas have been extensively studied on Hawaii, since the volcanic activity there is continuous and accessible. Hawaiian names have been given to various types of lava. A fluid kind flows easily and cools with a smooth billowy or ropy surface; this is termed *pahoehoe*. Lava that cools with a rough, splintery, jagged surface is called *aa*.

Intrusive Rocks

GRANITE is a widespread intrusive rock that makes up the cores of many mountain ranges. Composed of potassium feldspar, quartz, and usually some mica or hornblende, it cools slowly and thus develops a coarse and uniform grain size. Different varieties of granite are named for the presence of specific accessory minerals present in small amounts. There is considerable evidence that granite forms due to the melting of sedimentary masses of appropriate overall composition. This process has been termed *granitization*. **Syenite** is similar to granite, but contains little or no quartz and is fine grained.

PEGMATITE is a very coarse-grained rock of granitic composition. Pegmatites are frequently the homes of giant-sized crystals weighing many tons (such as quartz, feldspar, beryl, and spodumene). Pegmatite crystallizes from solutions emanating from almost-solidified granitic masses. These solutions contain exotic elements that could not be accommodated in minerals crystallizing in the granite. These elements form unusual minerals in pegmatites. The list of accessory minerals is very long and represents numerous rare species.

DIORITE is a dark-colored rock containing much amphibole or biotite. Its texture is coarse grained, like granite, but its mineralogy is very different. Quartz is absent or nearly so, and the feldspar is chiefly plagioclase. **Granodiorite** is richer in potassium feldspar. Diorite containing quartz has yet another name: **tonalite.** A rock intermediate between syenite and diorite is termed **monzonite.** If the plagioclase in a diorite is very rich in calcium (between labradorite and anorthite), the rock is called a *gabbro*.

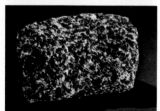

GABBRO contains pyroxene, as opposed to amphiboles in diorite. The primary feldspar present is labradorite, which has a characteristic blue color due to the optical effect Schiller (see p. 103). Gabbro therefore makes a very attractive building stone. Gabbro with very calcic feldspar (such as anorthite) is called **eucrite; norite** is a gabbro with abundant pyroxene and olivine. A gabbro composed almost entirely of anorthite feldspar is termed **anorthosite.** A fine-grained gabbro typical of small intrusives is called **diabase.** The most famous outcrop (exposed rock mass) of diabase in the world is the Palisades Sill, by the Hudson River near New York City. This igneous rock mass is hundreds of feet thick and lies amid sedimentary rocks that now dip gently toward the west.

PERIDOTITE is a rock composed primarily of the dark minerals pyroxene and olivine. If composed entirely of pyroxene the rock is termed a **pyroxenite;** if the chief mineral is olivine the rock is called **dunite.** An altered peridotite known as **kimberlite** is the host rock in which diamonds are found. Frequently the dark minerals of peridotite are altered to serpentine; rocks that have been extensively altered in this way are termed **serpentinite.**

Opposite: Granite (top l.), Pegmatite (top r.), Diorite. Above: Gabbro (top l.), Diabase (top r.), Peridotite.

125

Extrusive Rocks

RHYOLITE is a light-colored rock compositionally equivalent to granite. Some rhyolites show a flow structure that produces a banded or streaked appearance, indicating that the material moved while still molten. Sometimes material of rhyolite composition cools so quickly that crystals do not have a chance to form. The resulting rock, **obsidian,** has a glassy texture. **Pumice** has the same texture and composition but also contains numerous pores formed by bubbles of gas that formed in the molten rock. Varieties of obsidian that are brown and pitchy in appearance are termed **pitchstone.** Pumice will float on water because of the large proportion of open pore space it contains; large blocks of pumice may be thrown into the sea by volcanos and float far from their source.

PORPHYRY is a rock type that contains different grain sizes. If a magma begins to cool deep in the earth large crystals may form; the half-cooled rock may then be forced to the earth's surface and extruded, and the molten portion cools very rapidly resulting in a fine-grained texture. The overall rock therefore will contain both coarse and fine crystals, indicating its diverse cooling history. The fine material is called *groundmass* and surrounds larger crystals, called *phenocrysts.* Porphyries are named according to the groundmass composition (granite porphyry, syenite porphyry, etc.).

Above: Rhyolite (top l.), Obsidian (top r.),
Andesite. Opposite: Vesicular Basalt (top l.),
Basalt (top r.), Porphyry.

BASALT is a fine-grained, dark-colored rock. It is the most common and widespread volcanic rock and makes up huge volumes of crustal material in regions of extensive lava flows. The minerals present are too fine grained to be visible (a texture called *aphanitic*), but they include pyroxene, calcic feldspar, and olivine. Basalt (with diabase and gabbro) is favored for road building and is extensively quarried as *traprock*. Traprocks are the host for zeolite minerals in many parts of the world where surface waters have caused extensive alteration. *Amygdules* are almond-shaped gas pockets in basalts. **Scoria** is a porous, cinder-like rock sometimes seen at the tops of basalt lava flows. Basalt can be black, greenish, gray, or brown in color, but weathering usually produces a tan exterior rind.

ANDESITE is the volcanic equivalent of diorite. It contains little quartz but is rich in ferromagnesian minerals, and is therefore dark colored. Andesite porphyries are common. Andesite often resembles rhyolite, but the former may contain abundant olivine and pyroxene. The fine-grained equivalent of monzonite is called **trachyandesite,** or **latite. Trachyte** is the volcanic equivalent of syenite. **Phonolites** are trachytes that contain 10 percent or more of feldspathoid minerals.

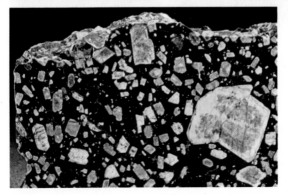

SEDIMENTARY ROCKS

About three-quarters of the rocks exposed at the earth's surface are sedimentary. They form by the deposition of particles of various sizes, or by the precipitation of chemicals in water. Some sedimentary rocks are made up of the shells of animals that have settled on the sea floor. The most distinctive feature of sedimentary rocks is layering, called stratification. A *stratum* is a single sedimentary bed or layer (plural: *strata*).

Sediments consist either of rock and mineral fragments, or of the mineral and chemical weathering products of these materials. **Mechanical** or **detrital** sediments include sand, gravel, clay, silt, and mud. Rocks formed from deposits of rock and mineral fragments have a *clastic* (broken) texture. In order of decreasing size, clastic sediments are termed boulders (over 10 inches), cobbles, pebbles, granules, sand, silt, and clay. Clay particles are microscopic. These materials become rock through various processes of *consolidation*, or *lithification*. In *compaction* the pore space between grains is reduced by pressure from the weight of overlying sediments. *Desiccation* is the drying out of water in pore spaces. Only fine particles are consolidated in these ways. In beds of larger particles there is sufficient space for access of solutions carrying dissolved minerals such as silica or iron oxides. These fill the pore spaces and remain when the solutions evaporate, thus cementing the sediments together.

Chemical sedimentary rocks are formed by the crystallization of minerals in solution, as in sea water. The most abundant rocks formed in this way are limestone and dolomite, made of the minerals calcite and dolomite respectively. (Dolomite actually is a mineral name, but large beds of the mineral are considered rock; this is an example of a rock made of a single mineral.) **Evaporites** are sedimentary rocks formed by the evaporation of sea water. Halite, anhydrite, and gypsum

Layered sedimentary rock exposures of Grand Canyon (above). Chert nodules weathering out of limestone (opposite) near Garrison, Utah, clearly reveal bedding.

are the principal evaporite minerals and may form very extensive deposits. **Coal** is a rock made of the remains of plants that lived millions of years ago.

Sedimentary rocks can form on dry land, where wind or glaciers deposit rock and mineral particles. Stream deposits also form characteristic sedimentary rocks. Rocks made of volcanic fragments are called *pyroclastic* ("broken by fire"). Airborne particles produce a fine-grained deposit called *loess*. Marine sediments contain the remains of animals that lived at the time the sediments accumulated. Sedimentary rocks are thus the likeliest place to find fossils—indications of former life.

Mechanical Sedimentary Rocks

CONGLOMERATE is a rock made of gravel or boulder-sized particles that have been rounded by tumbling about in streams or at seashores. If the fragments are freshly broken and therefore not rounded, the rock is called a **breccia.** **Tillite** is a conglomerate made up of fragments deposited by glaciers. The larger fragments in a conglomerate or breccia are usually rocks, while the smaller particles are minerals derived from other rocks. The chief characteristic of these coarse fragmental rocks is that they are *unsorted,* that is, they contain particles of various sizes mixed together.

SANDSTONE is made of particles of sand size (between $1/16$ of a millimeter and 2 millimeters in diameter). Sandstone is distinguished by particle size alone, not by composition. Thus quartz sandstone is merely one variety, made up of sand-size grains of quartz. **Arkose** is a sandstone composed principally of feldspar and quartz grains. **Greywacke** is a dense sandstone containing rock fragments and clay particles. Sandstones are typically cemented together with quartz, calcite, or iron oxide. A very pure, white sandstone made of quartz grains and cemented by quartz is called **orthoquartzite.** An example is the St. Peter sandstone, near Beloit, Wisconsin. Iron-oxide cement colors a sandstone red and is responsible for many of the bright colors of "painted deserts."

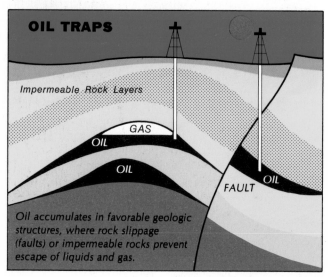

OIL TRAPS

Impermeable Rock Layers

GAS

OIL

OIL

FAULT

OIL

Oil accumulates in favorable geologic structures, where rock slippage (faults) or impermeable rocks prevent escape of liquids and gas.

Opposite: Conglomerate (top),
Breccia (middle l.), Red Shale (middle r.),
Cross-bedded Sandstone.

SHALE is a fine-grained sedimentary rock composed of clay or silt-sized particles. The **mudstones** have a blocky appearance, while **shales** split into platy slabs. The tendency to split along planes is the distinguishing feature of shales. Clay particles are actually flat plates, and compression into rock aligns these tiny crystals so that they lie horizontally. In sediments such alignment is called *bedding*. The stratification in sedimentary rocks is due to accentuation of bedding planes. Dating of sedimentary beds is based on known deposition rates and relationships between rock units. The matching of rock units of similar age is called *stratigraphic correlation*.

Shales sometimes contain sand particles and tiny crystals of other minerals. Shales may be gray, black, red, brown, or green; individual particles in them are too small to be seen with the naked eye.

The fine-grained quality of shale and clay allows them to act as barriers to the flow of water and other liquids. Thus arch-shaped beds of shale may trap water or petroleum and thus form valuable deposits. Shale is used in making cement, and clay is a valuable raw material in the manufacture of ceramics.

131

Chemical Sedimentary Rocks

LIMESTONES, composed chiefly of the mineral calcite, are the most abundant chemical sedimentary rocks. Most limestones form in the sea from the accumulated remains of marine organisms. Reefs are examples of such accumulations, built by such animals as algae, mollusks, and corals. These limestones are said to form biochemically. Most limestones are white, but they can also be black or gray and strongly resemble basalt. A good way to tell the difference is with dilute hydrochloric acid. Limestone, made up of calcite, fizzes in acid, whereas volcanic rocks do not.

COQUINA is a limestone made up of loosely cemented shells and shell fragments. The name comes from a Spanish word for shellfish. **Chalk** (from the Latin word *calx,* meaning "lime") consists of both tiny marine plant and animal skeletons and partly of biochemically deposited calcite.

DOLOMITE is a massive sedimentary rock composed primarily of the mineral dolomite. Many geologists currently believe that dolomite forms by the alteration of calcite (limestone) due to magnesium-bearing solutions. Limestone rich in clay is called **marl,** which may also contain abundant silica.

OOLITIC LIMESTONE is composed of small, spherical particles with concentric structures, called **oolites.** Oolites form by precipitation of calcite around a nucleus of some foreign particle, such as a sand grain or a bit of shell. **Pisolites** are similar but larger in size and may form **pisolitic limestones.** Some popular building stones contain oolites.

TRAVERTINE or **DRIPSTONE** is limestone formed in caves by the evaporation of solutions. Porous travertine is called **calcareous tufa.** The name "tufa" comes from the Italian for "soft rock," since this material is often porous and spongy in texture. Tufa forms by the precipitation of calcite from water in springs and streams.

GEYSERITE or **SILICEOUS SINTER** is a loose or compact siliceous deposit around some hot springs and geysers. It often forms crusts and is due to evaporation of hot-spring waters. It occasionally forms from the waste products of algae.

DIATOMITE (diatomaceous earth) is a chalky, white, powdery or compact rock composed of the shells of tiny single-celled organisms called *diatoms*. These accumulate at the sea bottom when the animals die, and can make up deposits of enormous extent. **Evaporates** are chemical deposits formed by evaporation of sea water; most of this material is halite. Hematite and limonite also form large chemical deposits, called "bog iron ore," which can be rich and valuable ore deposits.

Opposite: Coquina.
Above: Dolomite (top l.), Limestone (top r.),
Pisolitic Limestone (bottom l.), Geyserite.

133

Sedimentary Features

CONCRETIONS are masses of cementing material that have caused lithification of neighboring rocks. The cements may be silica, calcite, dolomite, or iron oxides, and concretions may range in size from less than an inch to several feet. They are often spherical, but can be flattened or elongate, and occasionally assume fantastic and complex forms. Concretions are sometimes harder than the rocks in which they form, and thus erode out relatively intact.

NODULES are masses of mineral matter—usually irregular and rough-surfaced—that differ in composition from the rocks in which they are found. Nodules are common in some beds of limestone and dolomite; they average several inches to a foot in diameter and are generally composed of silica in a form called **chert**. The nodules frequently were deposited at the same time as the surrounding limestones.

MUDCRACKS form when deposits of clay or mud are exposed at the earth's surface, dry out, and shrink. The shrinkage tends to pull the clay into polygonal (roughly six-sided) blocks. Loose clay and mud may wash into these cracks and harden. Mudcracks can only form in shallow-water areas where mud is intermittently wetted and exposed to the sun. In these same mud beds various types of impressions may be permanently preserved. *Raindrop impressions* are small pits that occasionally are found in lithified mudstones.

134

Above: Chert nodules in limestone.
Opposite: Concretions (top l.), Geode (top r.),
Fern fossil in shale (bottom l.), Mudcracks.

GEODES are hollow, more or less round objects, sometimes lined on the inside with glittering crystals that all point toward the center of the cavity. Geodes are commonly lined with quartz crystals, but they may also contain calcite, goethite, dolomite, hematite, and many other minerals. Geodes commonly occur in shales and are occasionally found in limestones and in volcanic rocks. Some geodes form by the gradual replacement of calcite concretions or nodules by silica, with the interior of the nodule dissolved out leaving an open space. This cavity may later fill with crystals. Geodes in sedimentary rocks form in this way. Geodes in volcanic rocks are produced by the filling of gas cavities by silica (to form a shell) and later by additional minerals. Geodes may be a few inches to many feet in diameter and many are spectacular and intriguing specimens for collectors.

FOSSILS are the remains of previous life. They are most frequently found in sedimentary rocks, because sediments offer the greatest chance for preservation of delicate structures. Organic remains of plants are buried and eventually become petroleum and coal. Sometimes leaf imprints are preserved in intricate detail in shales and limestones. The shells of marine animals are often hard enough to survive burial intact; sometimes they are replaced by silica or pyrite. The study of fossils is called *paleontology*. It is an important aspect of the general study of the earth's history.

METAMORPHIC ROCKS

Metamorphism derives from Greek words meaning "change of form." Metamorphic rocks have been changed through the action of heat and pressure on previously existing rocks. All kinds of rocks can be so altered—igneous, sedimentary, or even other metamorphic rocks. The chief result of metamorphism is a reorganization of the components in the altered rock. Minerals formed in certain conditions tend to be unstable in other, very different conditions; their chemical constituents tend to recombine in a form that is more stable in the new conditions. This is a process known as *recrystallization,* and its effects are displayed by most metamorphic rocks.

Metamorphism takes place within a solid rock (if the rock changes through melting, it can be considered igneous rather than metamorphic). Heat, pressure, and fluids are the chief agents of metamorphic processes. Heat makes the chemical components of a rock more mobile and allows them to recombine more easily. Pressure has the same effect, but primarily when it reaches the magnitudes expected at depths of over five miles (here the pressure of overlying rocks can reach more than 50,000 pounds per square inch). Fluids are mixtures of hot gases and solutions that are usually associated with magmatic activity. They promote recrystallization of rocks by carrying in solution the chemical species being reorganized in the metamorphic process.

Regional Metamorphism

Regional metamorphism takes place over extensive areas. It is classed as high-, middle-, or low-grade depending on the amount of rock alteration that has taken place. This is evident in the mineralogy of metamorphosed rocks. Certain minerals are characteristic of each grade, reflecting the conditions of temperature and pressure in which these minerals tend to form. Such minerals as kyanite, andalusite, staurolite, garnet, epidote, chlorite, and biotite are indicators of specific zones of temperature and pressure. One can determine the extent of metamorphism in a region by studying the mineralogy of the altered rocks.

Metamorphic rocks are classified according to their bulk compositions (which reflect the compositions of the original, unaltered rocks), and the temperature-pressure conditions of metamorphism. Even with the same overall composition, different conditions produce different alteration minerals. A grouping of specific minerals characteristic of a particular composition and pressure-temperature environment is called a *facies.*

Metamorphism tends to break and shatter minerals and spread them out in flattened layers; this is an effect of great pressure. The heat of metamorphism forces minerals to recrystallize and either form new minerals or, in the case of metamorphosed limestones, merely increase in grain size. Extreme flattening of mineral grains produces a texture called *foliation* (from the Latin *foliatus* meaning "leafy").

Metamorphism squeezes rocks until they bend or break.
Bent rock layers are called folds—as can be seen in this
well-defined formation on Canada's Gaspe Peninsula.

137

SLATE is a metamorphic rock formed by the low-grade metamorphism of shale. Intense pressure forces the clay minerals in the shale to align themselves in a parallel manner. Some of them recrystallize to form mica or chlorite, which are also platy and retain the parallel orientation. Slate containing abundant chlorite is green; black slate contains iron sulfides or carbonaceous material. The strong alignment of its mineral grains allows slate to break into thin, flat sheets. It is therefore a useful rock for roof tiles and walkways.

PHYLLITE is a rock that forms from slightly more intense metamorphism than is needed to produce slate. The grains of recrystallized minerals in phyllite are larger, producing a shiny appearance on broken surfaces. The rock splits easily with a characteristic "phyllitic cleavage."

SCHIST can be derived from any other type of rock, and so it is the most abundant of all the rocks formed in regional metamorphism. The recrystallized minerals—chiefly mica, talc, chlorite, and hematite—are large and well developed. Schist tends to break between layers of these minerals, producing a characteristic wavy or uneven surface. This property is called *schistosity*. Schists are named according to the minerals they contain. Chlorite and mica schist are derived from phyllite; hornblende schist and biotite schist are produced by metamorphism of basalt or gabbro. Quartz schist may develop from impure sandstones, and calc-schist from impure limestone. Schists may also contain such other minerals as feldspar, augite, hornblende, garnet, epidote, and magnetite. **Greenschist** obtains its color from abundant chlorite.

Above: Schist. Opposite: Phyllite (top l.), Gneiss (top r.), Migmatite (center), Slate.

GNEISS is a coarse-grained, banded rock resulting from high-grade metamorphism. It does not contain abundant platy minerals and therefore does not show a marked tendency to split along planes of weakness. In gneiss, the minerals are arranged in parallel layers, with quartz and feldspars alternating with dark (ferromagnesian) minerals. This layering produces the banded appearance. Gneiss (pronounced "nice") is named according to minerals it contains (hornblende gneiss, muscovite gneiss). **Migmatite** is a rock that forms when magma is injected between layers of a schist.

MARBLE is a coarse-grained metamorphic rock produced by the action of heat and pressure on limestone or dolomite. Under metamorphic conditions sedimentary carbonates dissolve bit by bit and recrystallize in larger grains. Pure marble is, like limestone, snow-white, but impurities in the original rocks can produce a variety of colors. Marbles, such as those used in building stones, can be colored green, red, brown, or black. Many have intricate and lovely bandings and mottlings.

QUARTZITE is a dense and compact rock, formed by the *induration* (hardening) of sandstone through quartz cementation. There are no pore spaces and when the rock breaks the fracture cuts across individual sand grains. In a sandstone, the break always follows the cement and bends around sand grains. Metamorphic quartzite is thus very distinct from sedimentary "orthoquartzite." Quartzite can be white, red, or various other dark colors.

ANTHRACITE is compacted and hardened coal. Metamorphism drives off hydrogen and other gases, leaving a residue much richer in carbon. Sulfur and various oxides may be present as impurities. Anthracite occurs in large deposits in eastern Pennsylvania.

Contact Metamorphism

Regional metamorphism may not always show obvious relationships to igneous bodies. **Contact metamorphism,** however, is the alteration of rocks due to heat generated by an intrusive igneous body. If chemical action occurs as well, the process is called *metasomatism*. The zone of contact metamorphism is termed a *contact aureole,* and may be from a few inches to many feet wide.

Certain minerals are characteristic of contact zones, especially in limestones and dolomites. These include graphite, spinel, idocrase, wollastonite, tremolite, diopside, grossular, and andradite. When large amounts of magnesium and iron are introduced by an intrusive body, such as a dike, the contact aureole is filled with masses of lime-bearing silicates. Such a body is termed a **skarn.** Many important ore deposits are associated with skarns and altered limestones. Contact aureoles are frequently zoned, with changes in mineralogy occurring at various distances from the intrusive. Contact effects are noted at most borders of igneous intrusions, even large bodies such as sills and laccoliths. A "baked" rock, typical of mild heat action on various rocks, is called **hornfels.**

Opposite: Quartzite (top l.), Anthracite (top r.), Marble. Above: Skarn rock.

MOON ROCKS

The moon has been a source of wonder and mystery since ancient times. Few details of the lunar surface were known until Galileo's pioneering telescopic work in 1610. Galileo described large dark areas that he called *maria* (seas), mountain ranges bordering the maria, and pitted areas he termed *craters*. Only one side of the moon is visible to the earth, since the moon rotates on its axis once in a single revolution about the earth. Nothing was known about the "far side" until photographs were taken by Russian and U.S. lunar-orbiting spacecraft in the 1960s.

In 1966 the Russian spacecraft Luna 10 landed on the moon and radioed back to earth data on the chemistry of the lunar soil. This information was verified by the results of the U.S. Surveyor 5 soon thereafter. The conclusion reached by scientists was that the lunar surface strongly resembled the familiar terrestrial rock, basalt, in chemical composition.

These initial findings were spectacularly confirmed by the results of the Apollo flights, which culminated in the first manned landing on the moon. The Apollo missions returned to earth carrying rock and soil samples from several areas on the moon. These samples are among the most intensively studied materials in the history of science. Although they do not represent all parts of the moon, they give a fairly good idea of what the moon is made of.

The moon is very dry. There is no free water (or ice) and even the minerals are all anhydrous. About 25 minerals have been identified in lunar rocks, including some that do not occur on the earth (armalcolite and pyroxferroite). The lunar rocks are similar to terrestrial basalts, but have exotic compositions due to crystallization conditions not found on the earth. In addition to basalts, a common rock type on the moon is breccia, made of fragments of other lunar rocks. These breccias are intensely fragmented, indicating that the surface of the moon is continually bombarded by meteorites of all sizes.

Another component in the upper layers of the moon's surface is glass. This material is rather abundant and is believed to be caused by the instantaneous melting of lunar rocks by meteorite impacts. The glass forms tiny spheres and also covers lunar rocks in the form of a crust.

The age of the moon has long been a matter of interest to scientists. Rocks brought back from the moon have proved to be older than any found on the earth. The oldest give dates of 4.4 billion years. Much still remains to be learned about the earth's only satellite, but lunar exploration (considered science fiction a decade ago) has become one of man's greatest adventures.

*Fist-sized piece of microbreccia, now on display
at Smithsonian, is one of the moon rocks brought back by
Apollo 11 astronauts Armstrong and Aldrin in 1969.*

TABLE OF CHEMICAL ELEMENTS

Element	Symbol	Atomic Number	Element	Symbol	Atomic Number	Element	Symbol	Atomic Number
Actinium	Ac	89	Hafnium	Hf	72	Praseodymium	Pr	59
Aluminum	Al	13	Helium	He	2	Promethium	Pm	61
Americium	Am	95	Holmium	Ho	67	Protactinium	Pa	91
Antimony	Sb	51	Hydrogen	H	1	Radium	Ra	88
Argon	Ar	18	Indium	In	49	Radon	Rn	86
Arsenic	As	33	Iodine	I	53	Rhenium	Re	75
Astatine	At	85	Iridium	Ir	77	Rhodium	Rh	45
Barium	Ba	56	Iron	Fe	26	Rubidium	Rb	37
Berkelium	Bk	97	Krypton	Kr	36	Ruthenium	Ru	44
Beryllium	Be	4	Lanthanum	La	57	Samarium	Sm	62
Bismuth	Bi	83	Lawrencium	Lr	103	Scandium	Sc	21
Boron	B	5	Lead	Pb	82	Selenium	Se	34
Bromine	Br	35	Lithium	Li	3	Silicon	Si	14
Cadmium	Cd	48	Lutetium	Lu	71	Silver	Ag	47
Calcium	Ca	20	Magnesium	Mg	12	Sodium	Na	11
Californium	Cf	98	Manganese	Mn	25	Strontium	Sr	38
Carbon	C	6	Mendelevium	Md	101	Sulfur	S	16
Cerium	Ce	58	Mercury	Hg	80	Tantalum	Ta	73
Cesium	Cs	55	Molybdenum	Mo	42	Technetium	Tc	43
Chlorine	Cl	17	Neodymium	Nd	60	Tellurium	Te	52
Chromium	Cr	24	Neon	Ne	10	Terbium	Tb	65
Cobalt	Co	27	Neptunium	Np	93	Thallium	Tl	81
Copper	Cu	29	Nickel	Ni	28	Thorium	Th	90
Curium	Cm	96	Niobium			Thulium	Tm	69
Dysprosium	Dy	66	(Columbium)	Nb	41	Tin	Sn	50
Einsteinium	Es	99	Nitrogen	N	7	Titanium	Ti	22
Erbium	Er	68	Nobelium	No	102	Tungsten	W	74
Europium	Eu	63	Osmium	Os	76	Uranium	U	92
Fermium	Fm	100	Oxygen	O	8	Vanadium	V	23
Fluorine	F	9	Palladium	Pd	46	Xenon	Xe	54
Francium	Fr	87	Phosphorus	P	15	Ytterbium	Yb	70
Gadolinium	Gd	64	Platinum	Pt	78	Yttrium	Y	39
Gallium	Ga	31	Plutonium	Pu	94	Zinc	Zn	30
Germanium	Ge	32	Polonium	Po	84	Zirconium	Zr	40
Gold	Au	79	Potassium	K	19			

TABLE OF MINERALS

The tables beginning on the following page are designed
to help the collector obtain rapid information about
minerals he is likely to find or to see in collections.
Many tables exist in the literature of mineralogy for identifying minerals, but such tables (to be useful) require
volumes in themselves. The listing presented here is
merely intended for quick reference. Where the property
of a mineral is variable, an average value is given in
parentheses which may be considered a representative
measurement for the species involved.

Abbreviations

Lusters

MET—metallic	GSY—greasy	SKY—silky
VIT—vitreous	ADM—adamantine	SUB—submetallic
RSN—resinous	PLY—pearly	DUL—dull
	RTH—earthy	

Color/Streak

RED—red	GRY—gray	GLD—gold
YLW—yellow	BLK—black	WHT—white
GRN—green	RNG—orange	COL—colorless
BLU—blue	PNK—pink	VAR—various colors
BRN—brown	SLV—silver	——white or colorless
	VLT—violet	

Crystal Systems

IS—isometric	UN—unknown	RO—hexagonal
TE—tetragonal	HX—hexagonal	(rhombohedral)
OR—orthorhombic	MO—monoclinic	AM—amorphous
	TR—triclinic	

Refractive Index

OPA—opaque   VAR—variable

Name	Composition	Luster	Color	Streak	Crystal System	Hardness	Specific Gravity	Refractive Index	Page
Acanthite	Ag_2S	MET	BLK	BLK	MO	2-2.5	7.2	opa	...
Acmite	$NaFeSi_2O_6$	VIT	BRN	—	MO	6-6.5	3.5	1.82	93
Actinolite	$Ca_2(Mg,Fe)_5Si_8O_{22}(OH)_2$	VIT	GRN	—	MO	5-6	3.1	1.64	95
Adamite	$Zn_2(AsO_4)(OH)$	VIT	GRN	—	OR	3.5	(4.4)	(1.74)	79
Adularia	$KAlSi_3O_8$	VIT	COL	—	MO	6	2.5	1.52	102
Aegirine	$NaFeSi_2O_6$	VIT	GRN	—	MO	6-6.6	(3.5)	1.82	93
Agate	See Quartz								
Akermanite	$Ca_2MgSi_2O_7$	VIT	VAR	—	TE	5	3.0	1.65	...
Alabandite	MnS	SUB	BLK	BLK	IS	3.5-4	4.0	opa	...
Albite	$NaAlSi_3O_8$	VIT	COL	—	TR	6	2.6	1.53	102
Allanite	$(Ce,Ca,Y)_2(Al,Fe)_3Si_3O_{12}(OH)$	SUB	BLK	GRY	MO	5.5-6	(4.0)	(1.75)	89
Almandine	$Mg_3Fe_2(SiO_4)_3$	VIT	VLT	—	IS	7	4.2	1.83	87
Alunite	$KAl_3(SO_4)_2(OH)_6$	VIT	WHT	—	RO	3.5-4	(2.7)	1.57	...
Amblygonite	$(Li,Na)Al(PO_4)(F,OH)$	VIT	WHT	—	TR	6	3.0	1.60	...
Analcime	$NaAlSi_2O_6 \cdot H_2O$	VIT	COL	—	IS	5-5.5	2.3	1.49	107
Anatase	TiO_2	ADM	VAR	—	TE	5.5-6	3.9	2.6	...
Andalusite	$Al_2O(SiO_4)$	VIT	VAR	—	OR	7.5	3.2	1.64	86
Andesine	$(Na,Ca)AlSi_3O_8$	VIT	VAR	—	TR	6	2.7	1.55	102
Andradite	$Ca_3Fe_2(SiO_4)_3$	VIT	BRN	—	IS	7	3.8	1.89	87
Anglesite	$PbSO_4$	ADM	COL	—	OR	3	6.3	1.88	74
Anhydrite	$CaSO_4$	VIT	WHT	—	OR	3-3.5	2.9	1.58	74
Ankerite	$Ca(Fe,Mg)(CO_3)_2$	VIT	GRY	—	RO	3.5	3.0	(1.72)	67

		Luster	Color	Streak	System	Hardness	S.G.	R.I.	
Anorthite	$CaAl_2Si_2O_8$	VIT	GRY	—	TR	6	2.8	1.58	102
Anthophyllite	$(Mg,Fe)_7Si_8O_{22}(OH)_2$	VIT	BRN	—	OR	5.5–6	(3.0)	(1.66)	95
Antigorite	$(Mg,Fe)_3Si_2O_5(OH)_4$	GYS	GRN	—	MO	2.5	2.62	(1.50)	97
Antlerite	$Cu_3(OH)_4SO_4$	VIT	GRN	GRN	OR	3.5–4	3.9	1.74	75
Apatite	$Ca_5(PO_4)_3(F,Cl,OH)$	VIT	VAR	—	HX	5	3.2	1.63	77
Apophyllite	$KCa_4(Si_4O_{10})_2F\cdot 8H_2O$	VIT	COL	—	TE	4–5	2.3	1.54	96
Aragonite	$CaCO_3$	VIT	VAR	—	OR	3.5–4	2.95	1.69	67
Argentite	Ag_2S	MET	GRY	BLK	IS	2–2.5	7.3	opa	...
Arsenopyrite	$FeAsS$	MET	SLV	BLK	MO	5.5–6	6.1	opa	53
Atacamite	$Cu_2Cl(OH)_3$	ADM	GRN	GRN	OR	3–3.5	3.75	1.86	...
Augite	$(Ca,Na)(Mg,Fe,Al)(Si,Al)_2O_6$	VIT	BLK	—	MO	5–6	(3.3)	(1.70)	93
Aurichalcite	$(Zn,Cu)_5(CO_3)_2(OH)_6$	PLY	BLU	—	MO	2	3.64	1.74	...
Autunite	$Ca(UO_2)_2(PO_4)_2\cdot 10\text{-}12H_2O$	PLY	YLW	YLW	TE	2–2.5	3.1	1.58	79
Axinite	$Ca_2(Fe,Mn)Al_2BSi_4O_{15}(OH)$	VIT	BRN	—	TR	6.5–7	(3.3)	1.69	90
Azurite	$Cu_3(CO_3)_2(OH)_2$	VIT	BLU	BLU	MO	3.5–4	3.8	1.76	68
Barite	$BaSO_4$	VIT	VAR	—	OR	3	4.5	1.64	73
Bauxite	Al hydrates	RTH	BRN	—	AM	1–3	(2.3)	var	60
Benitoite	$BaTiSi_3O_9$	VIT	BLU	—	HX	6.5	3.6	1.76	...
Beryl	$Be_3Al_2Si_6O_{18}$	VIT	VAR	—	HX	7.5–8	2.8	(1.58)	90
Biotite	$K(Mg,Fe)_3(AlSi_3O_{10})(OH)_2$	PLY	BLK	—	MO	2.5–3	(3.0)	(1.65)	98
Boleite	$Pb_9Cu_8Ag_3Cl_{21}(OH)_{16}\cdot H_2O$	VIT	BLU	BLU	TE	2.5–3	5.05	2.04	...
Boracite	$Mg_3B_7O_{13}Cl$	VIT	COL	—	IS	7	2.9	1.66	...
Borax	$Na_2B_4O_7\cdot 10H_2O$	DUL	WHT	—	MO	2–2.5	1.7	1.47	71
Bornite	Cu_5FeS_4	MET	YLW	BLK	IS	3	5.07	opa	47

Name	Composition	Luster	Color	Streak	Crystal System	Hardness	Specific Gravity	Refractive Index	Page
Boulangerite	$Pb_5Sb_4S_{11}$	MET	GRY	GRY	OR	2.5–3	6.0	opa	...
Bournonite	$PbCuSbS_3$	MET	GRY	BLK	OR	2.5–3	5.9	opa	...
Brazilianite	$NaAl_3(PO_4)_2(OH)_4$	VIT	YLW	—	MO	5.5	2.98	1.61	...
Brochantite	$Cu_4(OH)_6SO_4$	VIT	GRN	GRN	MO	3.5–4	3.9	1.78	75
Brookite	TiO_2	ADM	BLK	GRY	OR	5.5–6	4.0	2.6	...
Brucite	$Mg(OH)_2$	PLY	WHT	—	RO	2.5	2.4	1.57	...
Bytownite	$(Ca,Na)Al_2Si_2O_8$	VIT	VAR	—	TR	6	2.74	1.57	102
Cacoxenite	$Fe_4(PO_4)_3(OH)_3 \cdot 12H_2O$	SKY	YLW	—	HX	3–4	(2.3)	(1.60)	...
Cakite	$CaCO_3$	VIT	VAR	—	RO	3	2.72	1.66	65
Carnotite	$K_2(UO_2)_2(VO_4)_2 \cdot 3H_2O$	RTH	YLW	—	OR	1–2	4.1	(1.90)	...
Cassiterite	SnO_2	ADM	VAR	—	TE	6–7	7.0	2.00	58
Celestite	$SrSO_4$	VIT	VAR	—	OR	3–3.5	3.96	1.62	73
Cerussite	$PbCO_3$	ADM	COL	—	OR	3–3.5	6.55	2.08	68
Chabazite	$CaAl_2Si_4O_{12} \cdot 6H_2O$	VIT	PNK	—	RO	4–5	2.10	1.48	107
Chalcanthite	$CuSO_4 \cdot 5H_2O$	VIT	BLU	—	TR	2.5	2.23	1.54	...
Chalcocite	Cu_2S	MET	BLK	GRY	OR	2.5–3	5.7	opa	46
Chalcopyrite	$CuFeS_2$	MET	YLW	BLK	TE	3.5–4	4.2	opa	47
Childrenite	$(Fe,Mn)Al(PO_4)(OH)_2 \cdot H_2O$	VIT	BRN	—	OR	5	3.25	(1.68)	...
Chloritoid	$(Fe,Mn)_2Al_4Si_2O_{10}(OH)_4$	PLY	GRN	—	MO	6–7	3.5	1.72	...
Chondrodite	$(Mg,Fe)_5Si_2O_4(OH,F)_2$	VIT	RNG	—	MO	6–6.5	3.1	1.61	...
Chromite	$FeCr_2O_4$	SUB	BLK	BRN	IS	5.5	4.6	2.16	60
Chrysoberyl	$BeAl_2O_4$	VIT	YLW	—	OR	8.5	3.7	1.75	59

Name	Formula								
Chrysotile	$Mg_3Si_2O_5(OH)_4$	SKY	GRN	—	MO	2.5	2.4	1.53	97
Cinnabar	HgS	ADM	RED	RED	RO	2.5	8.1	opa	50
Clinochlore	$Mg_3Si_4O_{10}(OH)_2 \cdot Mg_3(OH)_6$	VIT	VAR	—	MO	1–2.5	2.8	(1.62)	99
Clinozoisite	$Ca_2Al_3Si_3O_{12}(OH)$	VIT	VAR	—	MO	6–6.5	3.3	(1.70)	89
Cobaltite	$CoAsS$	MET	SLV	BLK	IS	5.5	6.33	opa	..
Colemanite	$Ca_2B_6O_{11} \cdot 5H_2O$	VIT	COL	—	MO	4–4.5	2.42	1.59	71
Columbite	$(Fe,Mn)(Nb,Ta)_2O_6$	SUB	BLK	BLK	OR	6	5–7	opa	..
Copper	Cu	MET	RNG	RED	IS	2.5–3	8.9	opa	42
Cordierite	$(Mg,Fe)_2Al_4Si_5O_{18}$	VIT	BLU	—	OR	7–7.5	(2.63)	(1.55)	..
Corundum	Al_2O_3	ADM	VAR	—	RO	9	4.0	1.77	58
Covellite	CuS	MET	BLU	GRY	HX	1.5–2	(4.66)	opa	48
Crocoite	$PbCrO_4$	ADM	RED	RNG	MO	2.5–3	6.0	(2.4)	72
Cryolite	Na_3AlF_6	VIT	WHT	—	MO	2.5	3.0	1.34	..
Cummingtonite	$(Mg,Fe,Mn)_7Si_8O_{22}(OH)_2$	VIT	BRN	—	MO	6	(3.0)	1.66	95
Cuprite	Cu_2O	ADM	RED	RED	IS	3.5–4	6.0	2.85	56
Cyanotrichite	$Cu_4Al_2(SO_4)(OH)_{12} \cdot 2H_2O$	SKY	BLU	BLU	OR	1	(2.8)	(1.62)	..
Danburite	$CaB_2(SiO_4)_2$	VIT	COL	—	OR	7	3.0	1.63	..
Datolite	$CaB(SiO_4)(OH)$	VIT	GRN	—	MO	5–5.5	2.9	1.65	84
Descloizite	$PbZn(VO_4)(OH)$	GSY	VAR	RNG	OR	3–3.5	6	2.26	..
Diamond	C	ADM	VAR	—	IS	10	3.5	2.42	44
Diopside	$CaMgSi_2O_6$	VIT	GRN	—	MO	5–6	3.3	1.68	93
Dioptase	$CuSiO_2(OH)_2$	VIT	GRN	—	RO	5	3.3	1.65	..
Dolomite	$CaMg(CO_3)_2$	VIT	VAR	†	RO	3.5–4	2.85	1.68	67
Dravite	$NaMg_3Al_6(BO_3)_3Si_6O_{18}(OH)_4$	VIT	BRN	—	RO	7–7.5	(3.1)	1.65	91

Name	Composition	Luster	Color	Streak	Crystal System	Hardness	Specific Gravity	Refractive Index	Page
Elbaite	$NaLi_3Al_6(BO_3)_3Si_6O_{18}(OH)_4$	VIT	VAR	—	RO	7–7.5	(3.1)	1.65	91
Enargite	Cu_3AsS_4	MET	BLK	BLK	OR	3	4.44	opa	55
Enstatite	$MgSiO_3$	VIT	BRN	—	OR	5.5	(3.4)	(1.75)	92
Eosphorite	$(Mn,Fe)Al(PO_4)(OH)_2 \cdot H_2O$	VIT	PNK	—	OR	5	3.06	(1.64)	..
Epidote	$Ca_2(Al,Fe)_3Si_3O_{12}(OH)$	VIT	GRN	—	MO	6–7	(3.4)	(1.75)	89
Erythrite	$Co_3(AsO_4)_2 \cdot 8H_2O$	VIT	VLT	—	MO	1.5–2	2.95	1.66	76
Euclase	$BeAlSiO_4(OH)$	VIT	VAR	—	MO	7.5	3.1	1.66	..
Fayalite	See Olivine								
Fluorite	CaF_2	VIT	VAR	—	IS	4	3.19	1.43	63
Forsterite	See Olivine								
Franklinite	$ZnFe_2O_4$	SUB	BLK	BLK	IS	6	5.15	opa	60
Gadolinite	$Be_2FeY_2Si_2O_{10}$	VIT	BLK	—	MO	6.5–7	(4.3)	1.79	..
Gahnite	$ZnAl_2O_4$	VIT	GRN	—	IS	7.5–8	4.55	1.80	60
Galena	PbS	MET	BLK	BLK	IS	2.5	7.5	opa	48
Gehlenite	$Ca_2Al_2SiO_7$	VIT	VAR	—	TE	5	(3.0)	1.67	..
Goethite	$HFeO_2$	RTH	BRN	YLW	OR	5–5.5	4.37	opa	61
Gold	Au	MET	GLD	GLD	IS	2.5–3	15–19	opa	42
Graphite	C	GSY	BLK	BLK	HX	1–2	2.3	opa	44
Greenockite	CdS	ADM	YLW	RNG	HX	3–3.5	4.9	(2.5)	..
Grossular	$Ca_3Al_2(SiO_4)_3$	VIT	GRN	—	IS	6.5	3.53	1.73	87
Gypsum	$CaSO_4 \cdot 2H_2O$	VIT	WHT	—	MO	2	2.32	1.52	75
Halite	$NaCl$	VIT	COL	—	IS	2.5	2.16	1.54	62

Mineral	Formula	Luster	Color	Streak	System	Hardness	S.G.	R.I.	Page
Hedenbergite	CaFeSi₂O₆	VIT	GRN	—	MO	5–6	3.55	1.71	93
Helvite	(Mn,Fe,Zn)₄Be₃(SiO₄)₃S	VIT	VAR	—	IS	6–6.5	(3.25)	1.74	..
Hematite	Fe₂O₃	MET	BLK	RED	RO	5.5–6	5.26	(2.9)	59
Hemimorphite	Zn₄(Si₂O₇)(OH)₂·H₂O	VIT	COL	—	OR	4.5–5	3.5	1.62	88
Heulandite	CaAl₂Si₇O₁₈·6H₂O	PLY	VAR	—	MO	3.5–4	2.19	1.49	107
Hornblende	(Ca,Na)₂₋₃(Mg,Fe,Al)₅Si₈O₂₂(OH)₂	VIT	BLK	—	MO	5–6	3.2	(1.67)	95
Huebnerite	(Mn,Fe)WO₄	SUB	BRN	BRN	MO	5	7.0	(2.25)	80
Hyalophane	(K,Ba)Al(Al,Si)₃O₈	VIT	COL	—	MO	6	2.8	1.54	103
Hypersthene	MgSiO₃	VIT	VAR	—	OR	5–6	3.5	(1.70)	92
Idocrase	Ca₁₀Mg₂Al₄(SiO₄)₅(Si₂O₇)₂(OH)₂	VIT	VAR	—	TE	6.5	(3.5)	(1.72)	88
Ilmenite	FeTiO₃	SUB	BLK	BRN	RO	5.5–6	4.7	opa	..
Ilvaite	CaFe₃(SiO₄)₂(OH)	SUB	BLK	BLK	OR	5.5–6	4.0	1.91	..
Jadeite	NaAlSi₂O₆	VIT	VAR	—	MO	6.5–7	3.4	1.66	93
Jamesonite	Pb₄FeSb₆S₁₄	MET	GRY	BLK	MO	2–3	(5.8)	opa	..
Jarosite	KFe₃(SO₄)₂(OH)₆	VIT	BRN	YLW	RO	3	3.2	1.82	..
Kaolinite	Al₄Si₄O₁₀(OH)₈	DUL	WHT	—	MO	2–2.5	2.6	1.56	97
Kermesite	Sb₂S₂O	ADM	RED	—	MO	1–1.5	4.68	2.75	..
Kernite	Na₂B₄O₇·4H₂O	VIT	COL	—	MO	3	1.95	1.47	71
Kyanite	Al₂O(SiO₄)	VIT	BLU	—	TR	5–7	(3.6)	1.72	86
Labradorite	(Ca,Na)Al₂Si₂O₈	VIT	GRY	—	TR	6	2.71	1.56	102
Laumontite	CaAl₂Si₄O₁₂·4H₂O	VIT	WHT	—	MO	4	2.28	1.52	..
Lazulite	(Mg,Fe)Al₂(PO₄)₂(OH)₂	VIT	BLU	—	MO	5–5.5	3.0	1.64	..
Lazurite	(Na,Ca)₈(Al,Si)₁₂O₂₄(S,SO₄)	VIT	BLU	—	IS	5–5.5	2.4	1.50	104
Legrandite	Zn₂AsO₄(OH)·H₂O	VIT	YLW	—	MO	5	4.01	(1.69)	..

Name	Composition	Luster	Color	Streak	Crystal System	Hardness	Specific Gravity	Refractive Index	Page
Lepidolite	$K(Li,Al)_3(AlSi_3O_{10})(OH)_2$	PLY	PNK	—	MO	2.5–4	(2.9)	(1.57)	98
Leucite	$KAlSi_2O_6$	DUL	WHT	—	TE	5.5–6	2.5	1.51	104
Limonite	$FeO(OH)$	RTH	BRN	YLW	AM	5–5.5	(3.8)	2.05	61
Magnesite	$MgCO_3$	DUL	WHT	—	RO	3.5–5	(3.1)	1.70	...
Magnetite	$FeFe_2O_4$	MET	BLK	BLK	IS	6	5.18	opa	60
Malachite	$Cu_2(CO_3)(OH)_2$	VAR	GRN	GRN	MO	3.5–4	4.0	1.88	68
Manganite	$MnO(OH)$	SUB	BLK	BRN	OR	4	4.3	opa	61
Marcasite	FeS_2	MET	YLW	BLK	OR	6.5	4.89	opa	53
Margarite	$CaAl_2(Al_2Si_2)O_{10}(OH)_2$	PLY	VAR	—	MO	3.5–5	3.0	1.65	98
Marialite	$3Na(AlSi_3O_8)\cdot NaCl$	VIT	WHT	—	TE	5.5–6	2.60	1.55	105
Microcline	$KAlSi_3O_8$	VIT	VAR	—	TR	6	(2.55)	1.53	102
Microlite	$(Na,Ca)_2(Ta,Nb)_2O_6(O,OH,F)$	RSN	BRN	—	IS	5.5	(5.52)	(1.96)	...
Millerite	NiS	MET	YLW	GRN	RO	3–3.5	5.5	opa	49
Mimetite	$Pb_5Cl(AsO_4)_3$	RSN	VAR	—	HX	3.5	(7.1)	2.12	77
Molybdenite	MoS_2	MET	BLK	GRN	HX	1–1.5	(4.70)	opa	...
Monazite	$(Ce,La,Nd,Th)(PO_4)$	RSN	BRN	—	MO	5–5.5	(5.2)	1.79	...
Muscovite	$KAl_2AlSi_3O_{10}(OH)_2$	PLY	BRN	—	MO	2–2.5	(2.9)	1.60	98
Natrolite	$Na_2Al_2Si_3O_{10}\cdot 2H_2O$	VIT	COL	—	MO	5–5.5	2.25	1.48	106
Nepheline	$(Na,K)AlSiO_4$	GSY	VAR	—	HX	5.5–6	2.60	1.54	104
Neptunite	$(Na,K)_2(Fe,Mn)TiSi_4O_{12}$	VIT	BLK	BRN	MO	5–6	3.23	1.70	...
Niccolite	$NiAs$	MET	PNK	BLK	HX	5–5.5	7.78	opa	...
Niter	KNO_3	VIT	WHT	WHT	OR	2	2.1	1.33	70
Oligoclase	$(Na,Ca)AlSi_3O_8$	VIT	WHT		TR				

Mineral	Formula								
Olivine	$(Mg,Fe)_2SiO_4$	VIT	GRN	—	OR	6.5–7	(3.8)	1.69	85
Opal	$SiO_2 \cdot nH_2O$	VIT	VAR	—	AM	5–6	(2.0)	1.44	101
Orpiment	As_2S_3	PLY	YLW	YLW	MO	1.5–2	3.49	(2.8)	51
Orthoclase	$KAlSi_3O_8$	VIT	VAR	—	MO	6	2.57	1.52	102
Pectolite	$NaCa_2Si_3O_8(OH)_2$	SKY	WHT	—	TR	5	2.7	1.61	94
Pentlandite	$(Fe,Ni)_9S_8$	MET	YLW	BRN	IS	3.5–4	(4.8)	opa	::
Perovskite	$CaTiO_3$	ADM	YLW	—	IS	5.5	4.03	2.38	::
Phenakite	Be_2SiO_4	VIT	COL	—	RO	7.5–8	3.0	1.65	::
Phlogopite	$KMg_3(AlSi_3O_{10})(OH)_2$	PLY	BRN	—	MO	2.5–3	2.86	(1.60)	98
Polybasite	$(Ag,Cu)_{16}Sb_2S_{11}$	MET	BLK	BLK	MO	2.5–3	6.3	opa	::
Prehnite	$Ca_2Al_2Si_3O_{10}(OH)_2$	VIT	VAR	—	OR	6–6.5	(2.9)	1.63	88
Proustite	Ag_3AsS_3	ADM	RED	RED	RO	2–2.5	5.55	(2.8)	54
Psilomelane	Mn oxides	DUL	BLK	BLK	VAR	5–6	(4.3)	opa	::
Pyrargyrite	Sb_3AsS_3	ADM	RED	RED	RO	2.5	5.85	(2.98)	54
Pyrite	FeS_2	MET	YLW	BLK	IS	6–6.5	5.02	opa	52
Pyrolusite	MnO_2	DUL	BLK	BLK	TE	1–2	4.75	opa	::
Pyromorphite	$Pb_5Cl(PO_4)_3$	ADM	GRN	—	HX	3.5–4	(6.8)	2.06	77
Pyrope	$Mg_3Al_2(SiO_4)_3$	VIT	RED	—	IS	7	3.51	1.71	87
Pyrophyllite	$Al_2Si_4O_{10}(OH)_2$	PLY	BRN	—	MO	1–2	2.8	1.59	97
Pyrrhotite	$Fe_{1-x}S$	MET	YLW	BLK	HX	4	(4.6)	opa	50
Quartz	SiO_2	VIT	VAR	—	RO	7	2.65	1.54	100
Realgar	AsS	RSN	RED	RED	MO	1.5–2	3.48	(2.6)	50
Rhodochrosite	$MnCO_3$	VIT	PNK	—	RO	3.5–4	(3.5)	1.82	66
Rhodonite	$MnSiO_3$	VIT	PNK	—	TR	5.5–6	3.65	1.73	94

Name	Composition	Luster	Color	Streak	Crystal System	Hardness	Specific Gravity	Refractive Index	Page
Rutile	TiO_2	ADM	RED	BRN	TE	6-6.5	(4.2)	2.61	57
Sanidine	$KAlSi_3O_8$	VIT	COL	—	MO	6	2.57	1.52	102
Scapolite	$(Na,Ca)_4(AlSi_3O_8)_3(Cl,CO_3,SO_4)$	VIT	VAR	—	TE	5-6	(2.7)	(1.58)	105
Scheelite	$PbWO_4$	GSY	VAR	—	TE	4.5-5	6.0	1.92	80
Schorl	$(Na,Ca)Fe_3Al_6(BO_3)_3Si_6O_{18}(OH)_4$	VIT	BLK	—	RO	7-7.5	(3.2)	(1.66)	91
Scolecite	$CaAl_2Si_3O_{10} \cdot H_2O$	VIT	COL	—	MO	5-5.5	2.2	1.52	106
Serpentine	$(Mg,Fe)_2Si_2O_4(OH)_4$	VAR	GRN	—	MO	2-5	2.2	1.55	97
Siderite	$FeCO_3$	VIT	BRN	—	RO	3.5-4	3.85	1.88	64
Sillimanite	$Al_2O(SiO_4)$	VIT	WHT	—	OR	6-7	3.23	1.66	86
Silver	Ag	MET	SLV	SLV	IS	2.5-3	10.5	opa	42
Smithsonite	$ZnCO_3$	VIT	VAR	—	RO	5	4.4	1.85	66
Sodalite	$Na_4Al_3(SiO_4)_3Cl$	VIT	BLU	—	IS	5.5-6	(2.25)	1.48	104
Spessartine	$Mg_3Mn_2(SiO_4)_3$	VIT	RNG	—	IS	7	4.18	1.80	87
Sphalerite	ZnS	RSN	VAR	YLW	IS	3.5-5	4.0	2.35	49
Spinel	$MgAl_2O_4$	ADM	VAR	—	IS	8	(3.8)	1.72	60
Spodumene	$LiAlSi_2O_6$	VIT	VAR	—	MO	6.5-7	(3.18)	1.67	93
Staurolite	$Fe_2Al_9O_6(SiO_4)_4(O,OH)_2$	VIT	BRN	—	OR	7-7.5	3.7	1.75	86
Stibnite	Sb_2S_3	MET	SLV	—	OR	2	(4.58)	opa	52
Stilbite	$CaAl_2Si_7O_{18} \cdot 7H_2O$	PLY	VAR	—	MO	3.5-4	2.2	1.50	107
Strontianite	$SrCO_3$	VIT	WHT	—	OR	3.5-4	3.7	1.67	68
Sulfur	S	RSN	YLW	YLW	OR	1.5-2	(2.07)	2.04	44
Sylvite	KCl	VIT	COL	—	IS	2	1.99	1.49	⋮

Mineral	Formula								
Tantalite	$(Fe,Mn)(Ta,Nb)_2O_6$	SUB	BLK	BLK	OR	6	(7.5)	2.30	..
Tennantite	$Cu_{12}As_4S_{13}$	MET	GRY	BLK	IS	3-4.5	(4.8)	opa	55
Tetrahedrite	$Cu_{12}Sb_4S_{13}$	MET	GRY	BLK	IS	3-4.5	(4.8)	opa	55
Titanite	$CaTiO(SiO_4)$	ADM	VAR	—	MO	5-5.5	(3.48)	1.91	85
Topaz	$Al_2(SiO_4)F_2$	VIT	VAR	—	OR	8	3.5	1.62	85
Torbernite	$Cu(UO_2)_2(PO_4)_2 \cdot 8\text{-}12H_2O$	PLY	GRN	—	TE	2-2.5	3.2	1.59	79
Tremolite	$Ca_2(Mg,Fe)_5Si_8O_{22}(OH)_2$	VIT	VAR	—	MO	5-6	(3.15)	1.62	95
Turquoise	$CuAl_6(PO_4)_4(OH)_8 \cdot 2H_2O$	DUL	BLU	—	TR	6	2.7	1.62	78
Ulexite	$NaCaB_5O_9 \cdot 8H_2O$	SKY	WHT	—	TR	1	1.96	1.50	71
Uraninite	UO_2	SUB	BLK	BRN	IS	5.5	(9.5)	opa	..
Uvarovite	$Ca_3Cr_2(SiO_4)_3$	VIT	GRN	—	IS	7.5	3.45	1.87	87
Vanadinite	$Pb_5Cl(VO_4)_3$	VIT	RNG	YLW	HX	3	(6.9)	(2.3)	77
Variscite	$AlPO_4 \cdot 2H_2O$	RTH	GRN	—	OR	3.5-4	2.57	1.58	78
Vivianite	$Fe_3(PO_4)_2 \cdot 8H_2O$	PLY	BLU	—	MO	1.5-2	(2.63)	1.60	76
Wavellite	$Al_3(OH)_3(PO_4)_2 \cdot 5H_2O$	VIT	GRN	—	OR	3.5-4	2.33	1.54	78
Willemite	Zn_2SiO_4	VIT	GRN	—	RO	5.5	4.0	1.69	84
Witherite	$BaCO_3$	VIT	WHT	—	OR	3.5	4.3	1.68	..
Wolframite	$(Fe,Mn)WO_4$	SUB	BLK	BLK	MO	5-5.5	(7.3)	opa	80
Wollastonite	$CaSiO_3$	SKY	WHT	—	TR	5-5.5	2.8	1.63	94
Wulfenite	$PbMoO_4$	ADM	RNG	—	TE	3	6.8	2.40	81
Wurtzite	$(Zn,Fe)S$	MET	BLK	BRN	HX	3.5-4	3.98	2.36	..
Zincite	ZnO	ADM	RED	RNG	HX	4-4.5	5.68	2.01	56
Zircon	$ZrSiO_4$	ADM	VAR	—	TE	7.5	4.68	(1.94)	84
Zoisite	$Ca_2Al_3(SiO_4)_3(OH)$	VIT	VAR	—	OR	6	3.35	1.69	89

Index

Picture references in italics

Rock, Gem and Mineral Classics from Geoscience Press

Stones: Their Collection, Identification and Uses. Second edition. By R. V. Dietrich. A practical guide for collectors, *Stones* offers advice on where to find particular stones and information on how they are formed and how they can be used for everything from tools to toys. Paperback $8.95, 208 pages, 79 illustrations, ISBN 0-945005-04-0

Crystal Quest I. By Marcel Vanek. A delightfully outlandish series of cartoons, depicting the trials and triumphs of mineral collecting. Paperback, $9.95, 96 pages, 89 illustrations, ISBN 0-945005-05-9

Emerald and Other Beryls. By John Sinkankas. Every facet of the ore of the rare metal beryllium is covered in this richly illustrated work. Hardback, $64.95, 700 pages, 222 illustrations, ISBN 0-945005-03-2

Amber: The Golden Gem of the Ages, Second edition. By Patty C. Rice, Ph.D. The definitive study. Hardback, $29.95, 289 pages, 223 illustrations, ISBN 0-917004-20-5 Paperback, $19.95, ISBN 0-917004-21-3

Gemstone & Mineral Data Book: A Compilation of Data, Recipes, Formulas and Instructions for Mineralogist, Gemologist, Lapidary, Jeweler, Craftsman and Collector. By John Sinkankas. Paperback, $21.95, 352 pages, ISBN 0-945005-01-6

Field Collecting Gemstones and Minerals. By John Sinkankas. The primer on how to extract, preserve, store and exhibit specimens. Paperback, $22.95, 397 pages, 133 illustrations, ISBN 0-945005-00-8

Sinkankas's Standard Catalog of Gem Values. By John Sinkankas. The standard reference for both rough and cut gems. Paperback, $17.95, 286 pages, 50 illustrations, ISBN 0-945005-02-4

Please ask your local bookseller to order our books for you or order them directly from Geoscience Press, 12629 North Tatum Blvd., Suite #201, Phoenix, AZ 85032, (602) 953-2330.

Joel E. Arem is a Ph.D. mineralogist, author, photographer, lecturer, and former curator at the Smithsonian Institution. He is the President of Joel E. Arem, Inc., a company specializing in gemstones, gem and mineral photography, consulting services and public education. He may be contacted at P.O. Box 5056, Laytonsville, MD 20882.